THE COCKSPUR ISLAND LIGHTHOUSE

A Witness to History

Cockspur Island Lighthouse
Courtesy of Allen Lewis of
the Friends of Cockspur Island Lighthouse

The Cockspur Island Lighthouse

A Witness to History

Robert A. Ciucevich

Cover Photos Courtesy of Sharon Lindsay and Frank Logue of the Friends of Cockspur Island Lighthouse.

ISBN: 978-1-959563-41-9

Published by Maudlin Pond Press
P.O. Box 53, Tybee Island, GA 31328
www.maudlinpond.com

Printed in the United States of America

Contents

Chapter One

The Island

Since the founding of the Colony of Georgia, Cockspur Island has played an important and continuous role in our Nation's military and maritime history. Its strategic location just inside the mouth of the Savannah River makes the island ideal for defensive and navigational purposes, for which it still serves today. Since the early 18th century, Cockspur Island has been the site of multiple fortifications, navigational beacons, a lazaretto and quarantine station, and a navy base. Today, it still serves as the location of the Savannah Bar Pilots' dock and a U.S. Coast Guard Station.[1]

Cockspur Island c1780

This c1780 map, a portion of *Sketch of the Northern Frontiers of Georgia* by Sir Archibald Campbell, illustrates the strategic location of Cockspur Island at the mouth of the Savannah River. The southeast end of the island provided an ideal anchorage for ships making the long voyage across the Atlantic Ocean from Europe. *Courtesy of the Library of Congress.*

General James Oglethorpe and the first group of settlers arrived in Georgia on January 30, 1733. Sailing up the Savannah River, they dropped anchor off Cockspur Island, which was then called "Peeper Island" by the English as it was the first island seen by vessels as they entered the Savannah River.[2]

John Wesley – the Founder of American Methodism, and his brother Charles arrived in America in 1736 with General Oglethorpe, who was returning from England with new settlers and supplies for the new colony at Savannah. The first place they landed was Cockspur Island, where Wesley said his first prayer on American soil. In his journal, dated February 5, 1736, Wesley wrote: "*We cast anchor near Tybee Island, where groves of pines running along the shore made an agreeable prospect, showing, as it were, the bloom of spring in the depth of winter.*" The next day, Wesley wrote: "*About eight in the morning I first set foot on American ground. It was a small uninhabited island, … over against Tybee, called by the English Peeper Island. Mr. Oglethorpe led us through the Moorish land on the shore to a rising ground, … we chose an open place surrounded by myrtles, bays, and cedars, which sheltered us both from the sun and wind, and called our little flock together to prayers.*" The settlers spent two weeks on Cockspur Island recuperating from the voyage before proceeding to the new colony.[3]

Wesley Monument c1950

This monument located near the southeast end of Cockspur Island commemorates the arrival in Georgia of John Wesley – the founder of Methodism, and the approximate site where he preached his first sermon on American soil. The monument was erected by the Georgia Society of the Colonial Dames of America "to Commemorate John Wesley's Association with the Colony of Georgia." *Photograph courtesy of the author.*

In 1759, Jonathan Bryan, Esquire received a Crown Grant of approximately 150 acres of Cockspur while a small portion of the island at the southeastern end "was reserved for the Use of his Majesty."[4]

Fort George

The first military use of the island occurred in 1761 with the construction of Fort George, which was named in honor of King George III. Designed by German military engineer William Gerard de Brahm, the fort was built at Cockspur Point on the southeastern end of the island. The fort was constructed using enslaved labor and featured a square blockhouse that was used as a barracks, magazine, and storehouse enclosed within a wood palisade. An accompanying battery was also built across the south channel on Tybee Island near the customs checkpoint and quarantine station – or "Lazaretto" – which was built in 1768 to support the colony's emerging participation in the Transatlantic Slave Trade. In addition to providing defense against Spanish attack, Fort George was also intended to enforce quarantine and customs regulations.[5]

Aside from the fort, Cockspur Island remained relatively uninhabited in the decades leading up to the Revolution. By the 1760s Savannah had become a busy seaport, making it necessary for the colony to appoint a river pilot to help guide ships up the Savannah River. In 1768 the pilot of the river – William Lyford, petitioned the provincial government for one-acre of land on Cockspur Island to build a pilot house.

The pilot house was built in-close proximity to Fort George - which by one account had devolved into a ruinous state by the early 1770s. Despite its condition, the fort remained staffed with a small garrison to issue signals to ships entering the Savannah River. The fort was dismantled by the colonists in 1776 because of its exposed location and the belief that it would not be able to withstand an assault by the British fleet.[6]

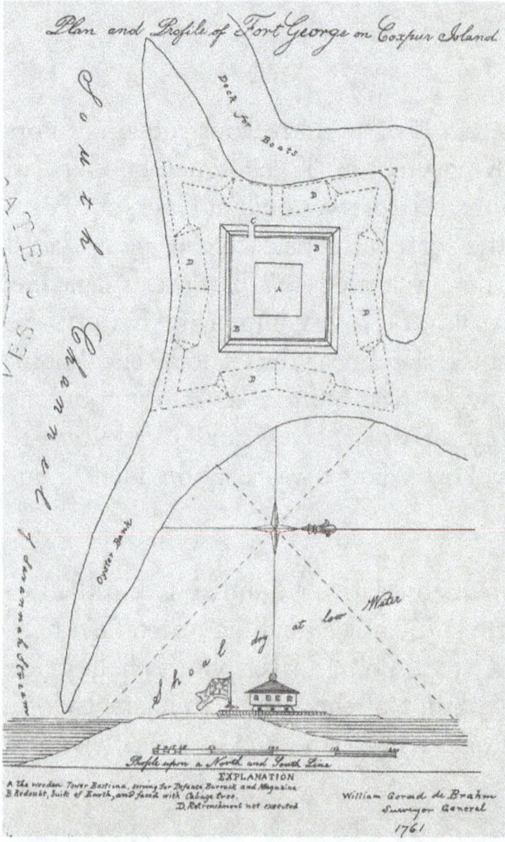

"Plan and Profile of Fort George on Coxpur Island" (deBrahm, 1761) – William Gerard de Brahm was a well-known cartographer and engineer who was commissioned by King George III to conduct a survey of the Province of Georgia meant to assuage the settlers concerns over the military threat posed by the Spanish in St. Augustine. In addition to Fort George, de Brahm built a defensive embankment around the perimeter of Savannah. de Brahm published a report on his findings in 1772.[7] Note the inscription "Shoal dry at low water" – an indication that the fort was located very close to the location of the Cockspur Island Lighthouse. *Image courtesy of the Georgia Archives.*

Blockhouse (c1750) – Fort Edward, Windsor, Nova Scotia, Canada (photo, lower right) The blockhouse at Fort George would have been very similar to this blockhouse built by the British in Canada around the same period. The blockhouse served as a defensive strong point for which the soldiers within a larger fortification could fall back to as a last resort. The blockhouse at Fort George was set within a 100 square foot earthen redoubt topped by a wooden palisade. Like this example, the blockhouse at Fort George would have featured loopholes on each side of the second floor that allowed defenders to fire in all directions.

Tybee Island was a refuge for loyalists during the Revolutionary War years (1776 – 1782) as a result of the protection that was provided by British ships that were moored off Cockspur Island. Many loyalists and their families fled to Tybee to escape the mounting anti-crown sentiment and to avoid persecution by the Patriots who had gained influence in the city. On the night of February 11, 1776, the royal governor of the colony, Sir James Wright, escaped to Cockspur Island where he was picked up by the British man-of-war *Scarborough*. Because he carried the Great Seal of the Province with him, Cockspur was officially, though briefly, the capital of colonial Georgia. It was from ships moored off the tip of Cockspur Island that Governor Wright, other officials, and British sailors ventured to the loyalist settlement that had developed on the north shore of Tybee to take on supplies, relax, and spend time ashore. In a letter aboard the Scarborough on March 26, 1777, Governor Wright recounted a raid on the loyalist settlement in which the Patriots had hoped for his capture:

> *Yesterday an attempt was made on Tybee Island, where the Rebels expected to find me on shore, with several officers and gentleman, but happily none were on shore from the ships, but four or five gentleman belonging to the town, who happened to be there, they took and carried away – some marines were also on shore cutting wood and a ship carpenter was there one of which was killed and three wounded ... and they burnt three dwelling houses.*[8]

Fort Greene

After the Revolution, Cockspur Island became the property of the new State of Georgia. With European threats intensifying, Congress approved the First System of American Seacoast Defenses, an act passed in 1794 that authorized the construction of forts to protect major U.S. coastal cities. Due to limited funding, most of these fortifications were built primarily from earth and wood and were soon considered inadequate in design. Through this system a second fort was built on Cockspur Island in 1794-95 called Fort Greene in honor of General Nathaniel Greene.[9] Fort Greene was "constructed of timbers and earth that were enclosed behind pickets ... and consisted of a battery designed for six guns, and a guardhouse constructed for the protection of the fifty-man garrison." The fort was located in the vicinity of the earlier Fort George, on the southeast end of Cockspur Island along the South Channel of the Savannah River.[10] Although intended to defend nearby Savannah, the fort was used primarily as a quarantine station. In 1804 a devastating hurricane flooded the entire island, destroying Fort Greene and killing half the garrison.[11]

In 1807 Congress authorized the Second System of American Seacoast Defenses to improve and expand on First System fortifications. The Second System – a program that was initiated between 1807 and 1815, resulted in the construction of fortifications having high stone or brick walls with multi-level tiers, internal casements, internal gun positions, and what were thought to be more appropriate designs for seacoast defense, such as star-shaped forts or other geometric shapes.[12] Rather than replace Fort Greene on Cockspur Island, the newly established Army Corps of Engineers chose a site farther up the river to build Savannah's new coastal defense. Fort James Jackson was built between 1808 and 1812 and was located one mile east of the city.

Fort Pulaski

Cockspur Island remained uninhabited and unused for several decades until the late 1820s when it was selected as the site for a formidable new fortification. Seaboard attacks by the British during the War of 1812 revealed weaknesses in the existing American coastal defense system, leading Congress to create the Board of Fortifications for Seacoast Defense in 1815 to develop a new comprehensive defense system known as the Third System of American Seacoast Defense. The Third System consisted of a chain of brick fortifications along the east coast of the United States that represented the premier coastal defense of its time.[13] Eighteen defensive works were identified for immediate construction and 32 projects were listed for future construction. Replacing obsolete First Order fortifications was a priority during the first decades of system implementation. As Fort Jackson was still considered a formidable defense, additional fortifications for the Savannah River were put off until 1821 when Cockspur Island was chosen as the site for a new fortification, to be named Fort Pulaski – after Revolutionary War hero Count Casimir Pulaski.[14]

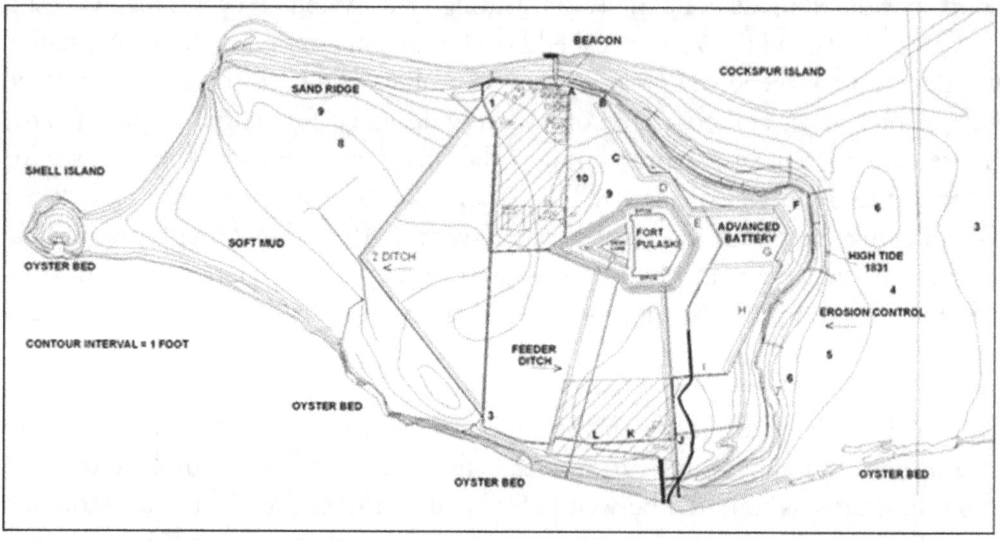

Cockspur Island, Fort Pulaski, and Fort Village – Based on a map submitted to the U.S. Army Engineering Department by Captain Joseph K. F. Mansfield November 1, 1843. *Image courtesy of the National Park Service.*

The federal government took control of most of Cockspur Island in 1830 when it purchased 150 acres from prominent Savannah businessman and plantation owner Alexander Telfair. The fort itself was to be built on the 20 acres formerly reserved for use by the Crown – and now owned by the State of Georgia, located at the strategic southeast end of the island. Construction of a worker's village, north channel wharf, and a system of ditches and dikes was begun in 1829 under the supervision and direction of Major Samuel Babcock of the Army Corp of Engineers. Later that same year, Robert E. Lee – a recent West Point graduate, was given his first military assignment as an assistant engineer under Babcock.[15]

Pulaski took 18 years to complete at the cost of 1 million dollars. Construction of the fort was made difficult by the muddy soil, which was drained and dried by the system of dikes that was built beforehand, as well as the swampy, wet conditions that promoted several infectious diseases that endangered the workers. The workman that built Fort Pulaski consisted of officers and enlisted men assigned to the post as well as skilled and unskilled laborers – which included enslaved Africans who were rented from local plantation owners. The fort is an immense five-sided, one-story masonry structure encompassing 9 acres – it and its demilune are enclosed by a moat. The fort features 67 casements with brick walls ranging from 7 to 11 feet thick. The casements served as gun galleries, quarters for officers and enlisted men, and for storage of ammunition and supplies. It is estimated that 25 million bricks were used in its construction. When it was completed in 1847, Fort Pulaski – with its intended armament of 146 guns, was thought to be indestructible.[16]

Fort Pulaski with North Channel of Savannah River in background. *Image courtesy of the National Park Service*

Slave Quarters – Hermitage Plantation c1907
"Savannah Grey" bricks manufactured by enslaved labor at the Hermitage Plantation were used in the construction of Fort Pulaski. Bricks delivered to Cockspur Island were brought in lots of one to seven million at a time. The hand-formed "rose brown" bricks were also used in the construction of many of Savannah's stately townhomes during this time. The row of brick slave quarters pictured above were all built using Savannah Grey brick, which often feature the hand or finger imprints of the enslaved men and women who made them. *Photograph courtesy of the Library of Congress.*

At the outset of the Civil War, Fort Pulaski had still not been garrisoned by the Federal Government, having only been assigned a caretaker and an ordinance sergeant. In January 1861, just before officially leaving the Union, the governor of Georgia ordered militia units to seize Fort Jackson and Fort Pulaski, Savannah's two main defenses. Located at the mouth of the Savannah River, Fort Pulaski was the principal defense of the nautical stretch known as Tybee Roads and the river approach to the city.[17]

In the summer of 1861, the Union had developed a plan to subjugate the South that included a naval blockade of key ports and the recapture of the southern coastal fortifications. A combined Army and Navy expedition set sail from Hampton Roads, Virginia. Referred to as "The Great Expedition," the force included a squadron of 51 ships and an invasion force of 12,000 men. Moving methodically down the eastern seaboard, the Union blockade reached Port Royal, South Carolina in November 1861. With the blockade only 25 miles away, preparations were made to defend against the impending invasion of Savannah by Brigadier-General Robert E. Lee, then commander of Confederate forces in Georgia, South Carolina, and east Florida. Believing that Fort Pulaski was a strong enough defense to keep Savannah secure, Lee ordered the abandonment of the sea islands of Georgia and the withdrawal of troops to the inner lines of defenses on the mainland. As a result, all Confederate forces on Tybee were evacuated on November 10, 1861. Because Fort Pulaski was believed to be invulnerable to bombardment from Tybee, the island was left undefended. It was thought to be unassailable for several reasons: it's seven-and-a-half-foot thick brick walls were impervious to long-range bombardment by contemporary ordinance; navy ships could not safely come within effective range of the fort without risking the concentrated fire of Pulaski's two tiers of guns; and because Pulaski was surrounded on all sides by the Savannah River and swampy marshes, there was no firm ground nearer than Tybee, a distance of one-and-a-half miles. Because it was generally accepted that smooth-bore guns and mortars did not possess the capability to breach heavy masonry walls beyond a distance of 700 yards, contemporary military thought dictated that erecting batteries on Tybee Island would serve little more than a preamble to a direct assault.[18]

"Fort Pulaski Under Confederate Control" – Harpers Weekly c.1862
Fort Pulaski was the principal defense of the river approach to Savannah and was considered virtually invulnerable to bombardment by both the Union and Confederate strategists at the beginning of the Civil War. General Totten, U.S. Army chief of engineers, declared, "you might as well bombard the Rocky Mountains as Fort Pulaski."

Unbeknownst to the Confederate war department, Union forces had developed a plan for the siege and reduction of Fort Pulaski from Tybee using mortars and a new weapon - the rifled cannon, which the Army began experimenting with in 1859. During a six-week period from late February to early April, 1862, a series of 11 earthwork batteries – mounting 36 guns in all, were constructed that extended a mile and a half along the north coast of Tybee from Goat Point to the Tybee Lighthouse. On the morning of April 10, 1863, the Union batteries on Tybee Island began a 30-hour bombardment of Fort Pulaski. By noon the following day, the walls of the fort were breached and the main powder magazine threatened, forcing the surrender of the fort a few hours later. While the long-range bombardment of Fort Pulaski was probably expected, the devastating effectiveness of the rifled cannons on the masonry walls at such a distance was unprecedented, rendering these types of defenses obsolete.[19]

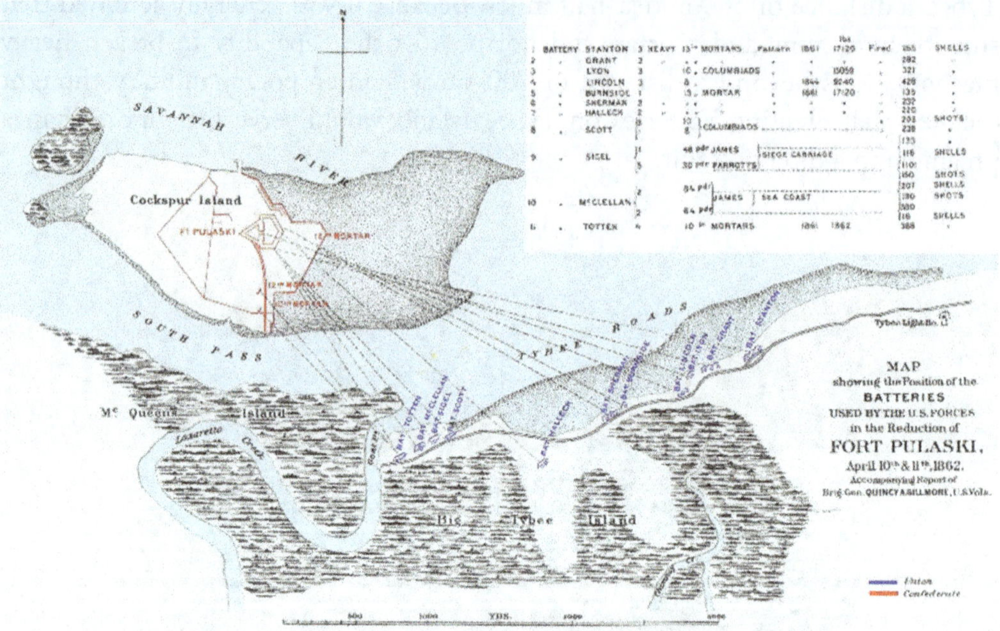

Plan for the Siege of Fort Pulaski – c1862 Brigadier General Quincy A. Gilmore drew up a plan for the siege of Fort Pulaski based on his knowledge of the successful tests of a new weapon – the rifled gun, which the U.S. Army had been experimenting with since 1859. Gilmore concluded that it would be possible to breach the thick walls of Fort Pulaski from Tybee using the guns. Work on a series of eleven earthwork batteries, mounting 36 guns in all, were begun on February 27, 1862. *Image Courtesy of the National Park Service.*

"Breach Side View" c1862
This famous photo by Haas and Peale depicts the devastating success of the rifled gun in breaching the masonry walls of Fort Pulaski, effectively rendering these types of defenses obsolete. Taken in January of 1862, the photo shows the breached southeast angle of the fort. *Photograph courtesy of the National Park Service.*

1st New York Engineer Regiment c.1862
Company F of the 1st N.Y. Engineers pose for a picture in the fort's Worker's Village. Company F were deployed to Tybee Island in February 1862 to prepare for siege operations against Fort Pulaski. This photo was taken around mid-April after the bombardment and capture of Fort Pulaski by Union Forces.[20] The building on the left is the commanding officer's office – the building in the center is the customs house. *Photograph courtesy of the Library of Congress.*

Soon after Union forces took control of Fort Pulaski, slaves from nearby plantations began running away to seek refuge at the fort. The Union blockade and its proximity to local plantations lead many owners to flee the coast, leaving behind the enslaved people who worked for them. Left unguarded, several slaves seized the opportunity to escape. The Union army put some of them to work as paid laborers around the fort while others assisted Union boat captains in navigating the creeks and rivers around Savannah. A few days after the battle for Fort

Pulaski, General David Hunter – a staunch abolitionist, issued an emancipation proclamation for all slaves on Cockspur Island.[21] A month later, he issued General Orders #11, declaring all slaves free in Georgia, South Carolina, and Florida. Although President Lincoln rescinded the order a few weeks later – preferring to reserve the authority to free slaves for the office of the presidency, Hunter's declaration is significant as it served as a precursor to Lincoln's own Emancipation Proclamation the following year.[22]

"Beacon Tower and Negro Cabin, Cockspur Island, Georgia" c1863
The photo above depicts a group of formerly enslaved who were living in the fort's construction village while working at Fort Pulaski – a few can be seen wearing surplus soldier's unforms.[23] The Union Army classified escaped slaves as "contraband of war" – or captured enemy property, and did not return them to their owners. This policy encouraged slaves to seek the protection of the advancing Union Army, creating a daunting refuge crisis and logistical dilemma. When Sherman's Army reached Savannah in Winter of 1864, they were accompanied by 10,000 former slaves. The issue of how to handle this humanitarian problem resulted in Sherman's famous "Special Field Orders, No. 15" in January of 1865, in which the sea islands would be reserved for the former slaves and each would receive "40 acres and a mule." *Courtesy of the Library of Congress.*

Following the end of the Civil War, Fort Pulaski was strengthened and modernized. Between 1869 and the mid 1870s, several improvements were made which included remodeling the demilune, installing underground magazines and passageways, and constructing emplacements for heavy guns. During this time, the Workers Village – which housed and supplied the garrison of soldiers and the civilian workers who maintained the fort and its system of dikes, had swelled to an occupancy level similar to the years when Fort Pulaski was being constructed.

Worker's Village c1863
A view of the worker's village taken from the northwest corner of Fort Pulaski. The large building in the center is the commanding officer's quarters, which served as a hospital during the Civil War.[24] Note the tall structure to the right of the commanding officer's quarters – this is the "fort beacon" depicted in the "Beacon Tower and Negro Cabin" photo on page 12. The fort beacon was located near the north pier to guide ships heading to Fort Pulaski to re-supply the fort and to drop off passengers. Unlike in present times, Cockspur Island was kept denuded of vegetation to make the fort easier to defend by making it less susceptible to a surprise attack. *Photograph courtesy of the Library of Congress.*

The officers lived in the Worker's Village officers' quarters and in other quarters with their wives and children, as well as their African American cooks. Civilian workers – which included skilled workers such as carpenters, blacksmiths, and masons, lived in the mechanics area of the village, while unskilled laborers lived in the laborers area. Enlisted men were housed in barracks situated in the demilune as well as within the casements inside the fort.[25] Cockspur Island had a population of 200 people during this time – twice the number of residents that the fledgling resort on Tybee Island would have during the early 1890s.

Additional modernization efforts were abandoned after plans were announced for the construction of a new coastal artillery post on Tybee to replace Fort Pulaski. In October 1873, the remaining garrison at the fort – the 1st U.S. Artillery, was withdrawn, leaving the lighthouse keepers and their families as the only inhabitants of Cockspur Island for several years. Fort Pulaski was officially taken out of service as a military post in 1880 but retained for its strategic location for future use by the federal government.[26]

U.S. Quarantine Station c.1890 - 1937

In 1884 the Fort Pulaski military reservation was turned over to the U.S. Army Corps of Engineers. With the quarantine station on Tybee badly damaged by a devastating hurricane in 1881, plans were made to establish a new quarantine station on Cockspur Island that would adhere more closely to national standards. In 1889 the War Department issued a revocable license to the City of Savannah to utilize a portion of the northwestern end of Cockspur Island to establish a quarantine. Construction of the United States Quarantine Station began in 1890. The station – which consisted of wharves, a hospital, store houses, and quarters for the Quarantine Officer, was in operation by 1891. In 1899 the Savannah station became part of the national quarantine system under the U.S. Marine Hospital Service, which was later renamed the Public Health Service.[27]

Quarantine Attendant's Quarters c2000
The buildings constructed at the U.S. Quarantine Station on Cockspur Island utilized the "West Indian bungalow-type of architecture." As introduced to Caribbean Islands such as Barbados and Guadeloupe during the 1700s, the one-story buildings were raised on wooden piers approximately 9 feet above the ground as a countering measure to extreme high tides as well as dampness, mosquitoes, and gnats.[28] The Quarantine Attendant's Quarters – pictured above, is the only building that remains of the Quarantine Station. After World War II the building served as the Park Superintendent's residence. The building currently serves as the park headquarters and administrative offices.[29] *Photograph courtesy of the National Archives.*

20th Century Coastal Defense of Tybee Roads and Savannah

As part of a nationwide effort to improve coastal defenses, the U.S. Army Corp of Engineers announced plans for the construction of a new fort on Tybee Island in 1872. In 1875, 205 acres were acquired by the federal government on the north end of Tybee for the establishment of a military reservation. The northern end of Tybee was chosen for its strategic location to defend Tybee Roads, Calibogue Sound, and the City of Savannah. Like Fort Pulaski and the "Third System" forts before it, this new fort – called Fort Screven, was one segment of a network of newly-developed coastal defense batteries conceived during the period of Caribbean and Pan American unrest of the 1890s and constructed along the Atlantic and Gulf Coasts to protect major cities and ports from naval bombardment and blockade. These Endicott Period or "Fourth Order" forts were designed to address the weaknesses exposed during the attack on Fort Pulaski in 1862 and to defend against the new military technologies of the day. This new system of coastal defenses was begun in 1897 in response to the mounting tensions in the region that would eventually lead to the Spanish American War.[30]

The first phase of Fort Screven was constructed from 1897 to 1904 and featured a battery of six poured-in-place, reinforced concrete gun emplacements that wrapped around the coastline of the north end of Tybee, forming a U-shape around the five-acre Tybee Light Station. Each emplacement featured its own set of catwalks and corridors that led to the ammunition magazine below. The batteries were buttressed on the seaside by large sand dunes and sand embankments to conceal their location and to serve as added protection for the magazines. Ammunition for the guns was raised to the firing platform by an elevator, and crew members used carts to wheel the shells to the guns. Battery Brumby, the largest of the battery complexes, was the first to be completed and the only one in service during the Spanish-American War, which only lasted eight months from April to November 1898. Battery Brumby featured four eight-inch rifles mounted on disappearing carriages and was manned by 4 officers and 157 men.[31]

While Fort Pulaski was no longer an active military post, Cockspur Island still served a key role in the defense of the key port of Savannah. Because the majority of the batteries at Fort Screven were still under construction during the war, Savannah's coastal defenses were augmented by an electronic minefield deployed in the north channel of the Savannah River and by the U.S.S. *Amphrite*, which patrolled between Savannah and Charleston. The minefield was operated by a small garrison stationed in the demilune area of Fort Pulaski. Each mine was attached to a buoy. A signal was transmitted to the garrison at Fort Pulaski each time a ship struck a buoy. From their vantage point on Cockspur Island, the observers at Fort Pulaski could determine whether the ship was an enemy vessel and, if so, could electronically detonate the mines to prevent it from entering the channel.[32]

In addition to the batteries on Tybee, a small, poured-in-place reinforced concrete battery like those at Fort Screven was erected near the Fort Pulaski pier on the north shore of Cockspur Island to protect the north channel of the Savannah River. Begun in June 1899, Battery Horace Hambright featured three subterranean magazines and emplacements for two three-inch rapid-fire guns.[33] When the battery was completed in 1903, the threat of regional conflict had dissipated. Because the main batteries at Fort Screven had been completed by this time, Hambright's armament was never installed.

Battery Hambright c2024
Of the seven "Endicott Period" concrete batteries constructed to defend Tybee Roads and Calibogue Sound, Battery Hambright -along with Battery Gant and Battery Brumby at Fort Screven, appears to be the best preserved. Unlike the Fort Screven batteries, Battery Hambright is the only battery that retains its original earthen embankments. The sand embankments that buttressed Fort Screven's batteries were removed during the 1920s to serve as infill during the construction of the Tybee Road. *Photograph courtesy of the author.*

During World War I, preparations were made for the U.S. Quarantine Station on the west end of Cockspur Island to receive German prisoners of war, but the war ended before the facility was used for this purpose.[34] The station was later expanded to include twenty buildings on a 130-acre campus. By the 1930s advances in the treatment of contagious diseases and a decline in immigration rendered the facility obsolete. In 1937 the Savannah Quarantine Station was closed, and the complex and grounds were transferred to the National Park Service by the Treasury Department.[35]

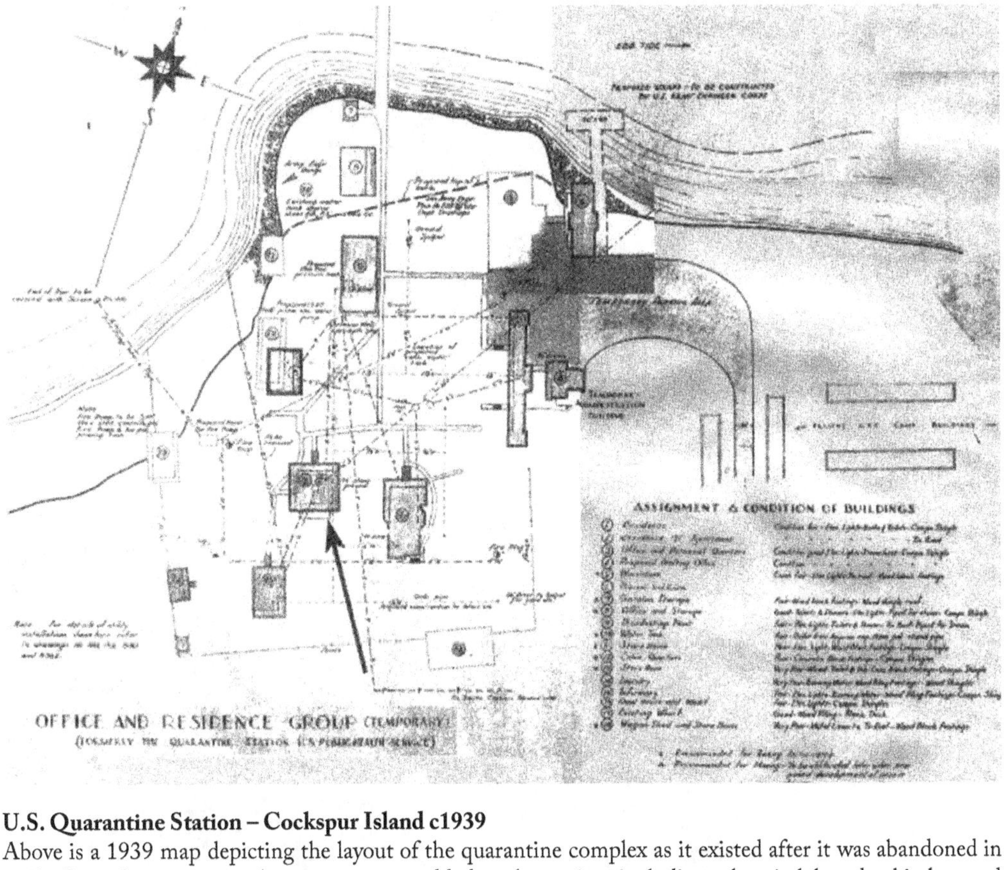

U.S. Quarantine Station – Cockspur Island c1939

Above is a 1939 map depicting the layout of the quarantine complex as it existed after it was abandoned in 1937. Over the years several structures were added to the station, including a hospital, laundry, kitchen and dining hall, sailors' quarters, fumigation building, and quarters for staff. As depicted on the map – Civilian Conservation Corps Camp 460 was established to the east of the quarantine station in 1934. The CCC was assigned the task of restoring Fort Pulaski, which was established as a National Monument in 1924.[36] *Image courtesy of the National Park Service.*

Moat Excavation c1935
During the 1930s CCC workers began the arduous task of reversing decades of deferred maintenance at Fort Pulaski. By this time the moat had filled up with silt and debris – the photo above depicts an excavator removing the decades of dirt that had accumulated. In addition to the moat, the workers were tasked with restoring the dike system that fed the moat as well as making repairs to the masonry fort itself. *Photograph courtesy of the National Park Service.*

Repairs to the Breached Wall c1935.
CCC workers repair the famous "breached wall" at Fort Pulaski's southeast angle. A different colored brick was used in the restoration of the outer walls in order to illustrate where the rifled cannons were most successful during the historic bombardment of the fort. *Photograph courtesy of the National Park Service.*

U.S. Quarantine Station, Cockspur Island c1937
This photo was taken from the North Channel of the Savannah River by Ralston B. Lattimore, the first Superintendent of the Fort Pulaski National Monument. After the Bureau of Public Health closed the station in 1937, the War Department transferred ownership of the site to the Department of the Interior. Lattimore's plans to redevelop the station for use by park staff was soon interrupted by wartime preparations as the U.S. Navy sought to adapt the old station into a U.S. Navy Section Base.[37] *Photograph courtesy of the National Park Service*

U.S. Navy Section Base c1942 - 1944

With the United States entry into World War II, the old quarantine station and CCC camp on the northwest end of Cockspur Island was requisitioned by the U.S. Navy for use as a section base for its Inshore Patrol. The base was intended to counter U-boat incursions along the coast. In March of 1942 the Department of Interior notified the National Park Service that Cockspur Island would be turned over to the Navy for the remainder of the war. Although Section Base #20 began operations on July 8, 1942, nearly $2,000,000 in new construction and alterations to the old facility was carried out by the Navy during 1942 and 1943. After D-Day – with the Germans on the defensive, operations at the base had nearly ceased. In September 1944 the base was decommissioned. In 1948 the Department of Interior returned Cockspur Island to National Park Service control.[38]

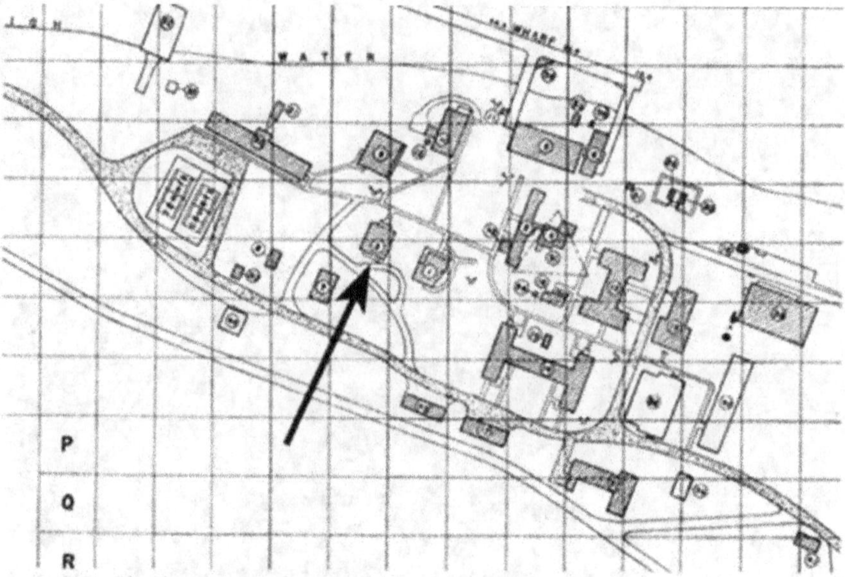

U.S. Navy Section Base #20 – Cockspur Island c1942-43
A detail view from a larger map entitled "Section Base, Savannah, Georgia, June 1942" that shows the former quarantine station and CCC camp as adapted and expanded for use by the U.S. Navy. When the base was completed, it included barracks that could accommodate up to 400 men, an administrative office, an air-cooled movie theater, club rooms and dining facilities, an officer's club, gymnasium, athletic fields, and tennis courts.[39] *Image courtesy of the National Park Service.*

Munitions Bunker, U.S. Navy Section Base #20, Cockspur Island, undated
The Navy commissioned the construction of a series of cast-in-place concrete bunkers at the west end of Cockspur Island for the storage of munitions and other supplies. The historic photo above depicts one of two bunkers utilized by park staff. Three other bunkers located nearby are owned and used by the Georgia Department of Transportation. The bunkers and an equipment storage building – which now houses the park's facilities maintenance department, are the only remaining structures associated with the Navy base. *Image courtesy of the National Park Service.*

Chapter Two

The Lighthouses

Since the beginning of the Colony of Georgia, the east end of Cockspur Island has served as an important navigational point for the port of Savannah because it separates the North and South Channels of the Savannah River. The first Tybee Island Lighthouse was built in 1736 to mark the entrance to the Savannah River, but mariners still had to sail seventeen miles upstream and circumvent several islands to reach the port of Savannah. While no beacon is known to have been constructed on the island during the 18th century, a pilot house was built on Cockspur Island for the "pilot of the river" in 1768, and Fort Green – located on the island's southeastern tip, was reported to have been staffed by a small garrison during the 1770s to issue signals to ships entering the river.[1] This early navigational significance is acknowledged by the U.S. Coast Guard, which lists 1772 as the year the light station on Cockspur Island was first established.[2]

The first indication that a traditional aid to navigation was to be built on Cockspur Island occurred in 1826 when Congress approved an appropriation of $1,500 to construct a beacon on "Grass Island" off the tip of Cockspur.[3] An 1827 study of the harbor conducted by the U.S. Army Corp of Engineers attests to the presence of the beacon by this time. The need for such a beacon – as well as the Corps of Engineers' study of the harbor, was certainly associated with the federal government's plans for Fort Pulaski. The southeast end of Cockspur Island was selected as the site for the new fort in 1821, and construction on the North Channel pier, dike system, and construction village was begun in 1829.[4]

In 1834, Congress approved an allocation of $4,000 dollars for the construction of two brick beacons on Cockspur Island – of which one appears to have been intended as a replacement for the earlier wooden daymark built in 1827. In 1837, a re-appropriation of $3,000 was approved by Congress, and construction of the two unlit brick beacons was finally begun. One of the beacons – the first brick tower built on the "islet" off the eastern tip of Cockspur, was intended to mark the entrance to the South Channel.[5] This was the Cockspur Island beacon. The other brick tower was the Oyster Beds Beacon, which was intended to mark the entrance to the North Channel. It was constructed on Oyster Bed Island, a small oyster shoal in the Savannah River.

Pulaski Beacon, Cockspur Island c1863
This photo, entitled "Beacon Tower and Negro Cabin," depicts a third brick beacon that was built on Cockspur Island near the North Pier as part of the construction village begun in 1829. Its octagonal shape is characteristic of early tower construction. Also referred to on maps as "Fort Beacon," the daymark is depicted on an 1843 Army Corp of Engineers Map of Cockspur Island and again on an 1855 survey map of the Savannah River, in which it is referred to as "Pulaski Beacon." A daymark is a navigational aid that is unlit – or lacks a lighting apparatus at its apex, as pictured above. Often referred to as a "beacon," these towers were not true "lighthouses" in the practical sense since they did not possess a Fresnel lens, but nevertheless made up an important part of the navigational system of local waterways. *Photograph courtesy of the Library of Congress.*

The Cockspur Island and Oyster Beds Range Light-Station

In 1839, the engineer of the Sixth Lighthouse District of the Savannah area wrote a letter to the Treasury Department –whose jurisdiction the operation of the nation's lighthouses was under at the time, indicating that the Cockspur beacon had been damaged in a storm shortly after completion and that it would need to be rebuilt. No action was taken until 1848 when W.B. Bulloch – Superintendent of the Lights in the Savannah area, wrote a series of letters to the Treasury Department regarding the construction of a new beacon tower for Cockspur Island, stating his opinion that it should be converted into a lighthouse. Later that year Bulloch sent the proposed plans to the auditor of the Treasury Department – Stephen Pleasonton, which included an estimate by noted local architect John S. Norris *"to repair, alter and put up Lantern and Lights on the Round Tower or Beacon* *on Cockspur, according to the plan, elevation, and specifications accompanying this for … $2,350."* Norris was later contracted to do the work which also included the *"erection of a suitable Keepers House."*[6]

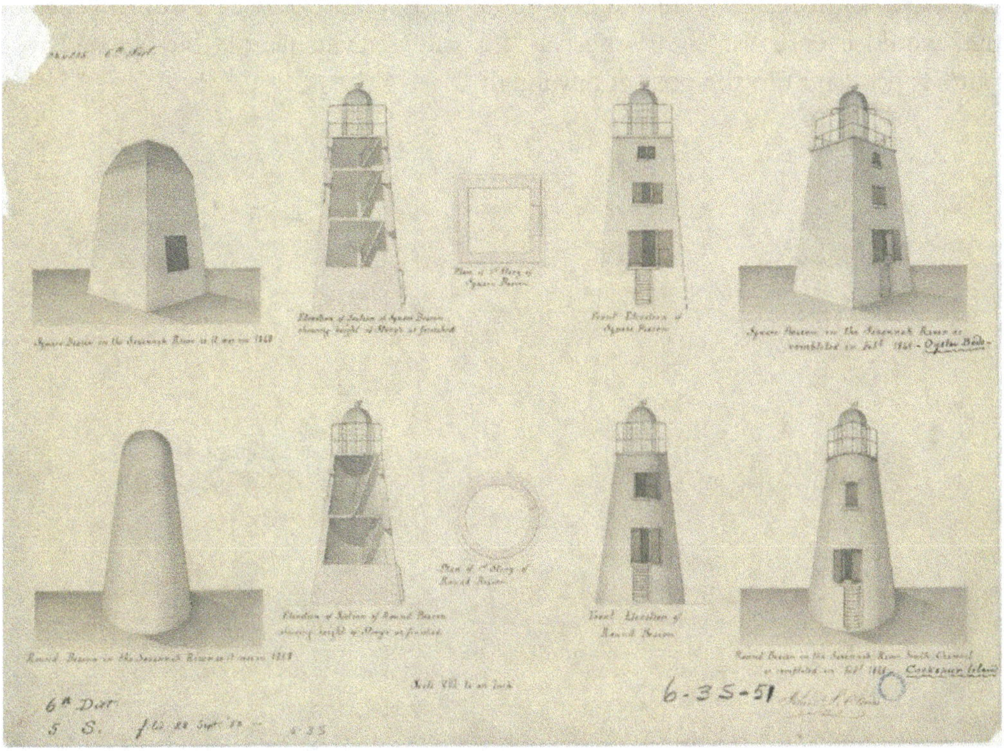

Cockspur Island and Oyster Beds Beacons c1837-39
Savannah architect John S. Norris prepared these "before and after" plans of the Cockspur Island and Oyster Beds Beacon towers as they appeared in 1848 – while still unlit brick daymarks (as depicted at far left), and after their conversion into lighthouses after work was completed in 1849 (as depicted at far right). Both beacons were clearly extant before this date, lending credence to the theory that Oyster Beds Beacon was one of the two beacons built by the Lighthouse Establishment between 1837 and 1839. *Image courtesy of the National Archives.*

Under Norris's direction, work on the rebuilding and retrofitting of the Cockspur Island beacon was complete by February 1849. According to Annual Reports of the Lighthouse Board, the lighthouse had a fixed white light which emitted from five lamps with 14-inch reflectors; it possessed a focal plane that was 25 feet above sea level; and it generated a light that was visible for nine and three-quarter miles at sea. While historic letters and accounts relate the funding, repair, and conversion of the Cockspur Island beacon into a true lighthouse, there is no such correspondence or documentation that the same work was conducted for the Oyster Beds Beacon, with the exception of Norris's c1849 "before and after" drawings that he prepared as evidence of the work carried out on both beacons at that time. Oyster Beds Beacon possessed the same characteristics as its counterpart, although it displayed a fixed red light and was square in shape – perhaps as a way of differentiating the two beacons when they were originally built as daymarks. These two lighthouses were the beginning of a system of over a dozen beacons that would eventually "light" the way for ships traversing the Savannah River from Tybee Light to the port of Savannah.[7]

Cockspur Island Lighthouse c1849
John S. Norris oversaw the reconstruction of the original unlit brick tower that was damaged by a storm shortly after its completion in 1839 – which is depicted in the drawing above. According to a historic structures report prepared by the Historic American Buildings Survey (HABS), the design of the 1849 lighthouse was prepared by engineers of the Sixth Lighthouse District, not by Norris himself. The distinctive "bird cage" style lamp room is clearly an indication that a Winslow Lewis-design was utilized or emulated. Lewis was a prolific builder and designer of lighthouses – he was awarded many contracts by the Lighthouse Establishment largely due to his ability to underbid other competitors. Lewis may have been awarded the contract to design the Cockspur Island lighthouse and make provisions for the lighting apparatus (which he designed and patented) while Norris was hired to supervise its construction (a common arrangement in lighthouse construction of the period). *Image courtesy of the National Archives.*

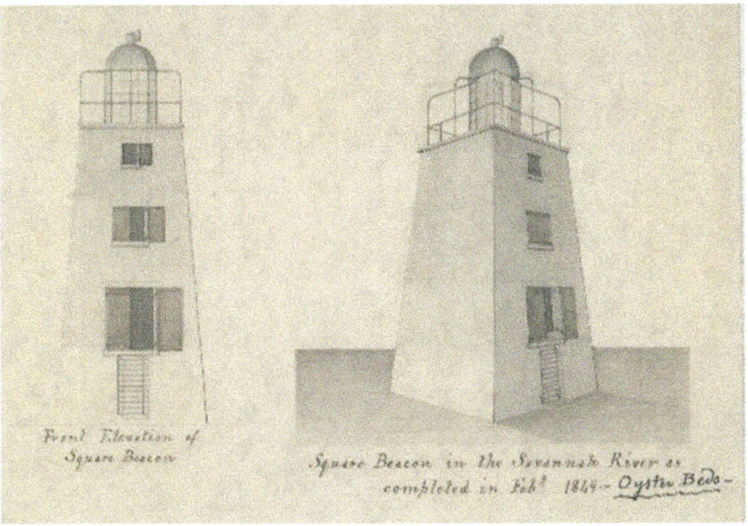

Oyster Beds Beacon Lighthouse c1849
The drawing above is the only known image of the Oyster Beds Beacon. The tower was built on a small oyster shoal in the North Channel of the Savannah River which is depicted on historic and contemporary maps as "Oyster Bed Island." Unlike the site of the Cockspur Lighthouse, which was located on a tidal islet that was originally accessible by foot during low tide, the Oyster Beds Beacon could only be reached by boat. *Image courtesy of the National Archives.*

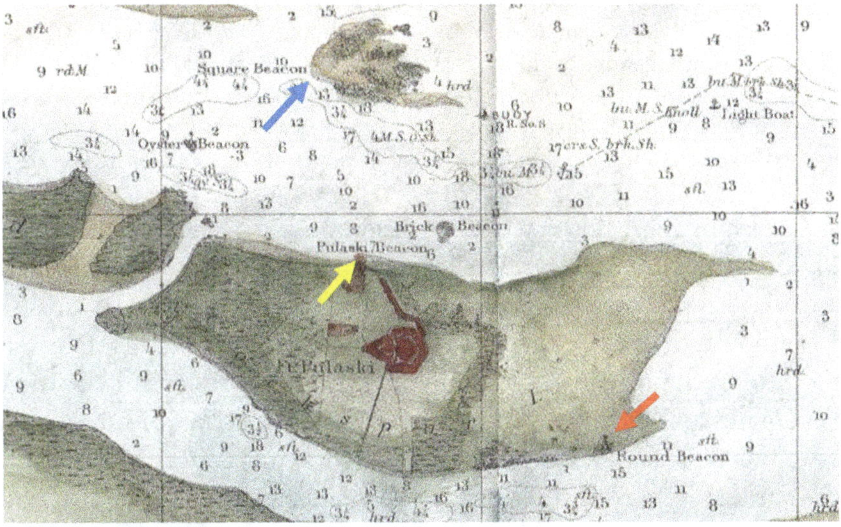

Cockspur Island c1855
This map of Cockspur Island, a small section of *Preliminary Chart of the Savannah River* prepared for the U.S. Army Corp of Engineers, depicts the Cockspur Island and Oyster Beds Beacon Light Station as it existed in 1855. The Cockspur Lighthouse (red arrow) is labelled "Round Beacon" and the Oyster Beds Lighthouse (blue arrow) is labelled as "Square Beacon." The tidal marsh surrounding the Cockspur Lighthouse is clearly depicted by a light green. Also labeled in the map is the "Pulaski Beacon," possibly built as early as 1829 (yellow arrow). *Image courtesy Geographicus.*

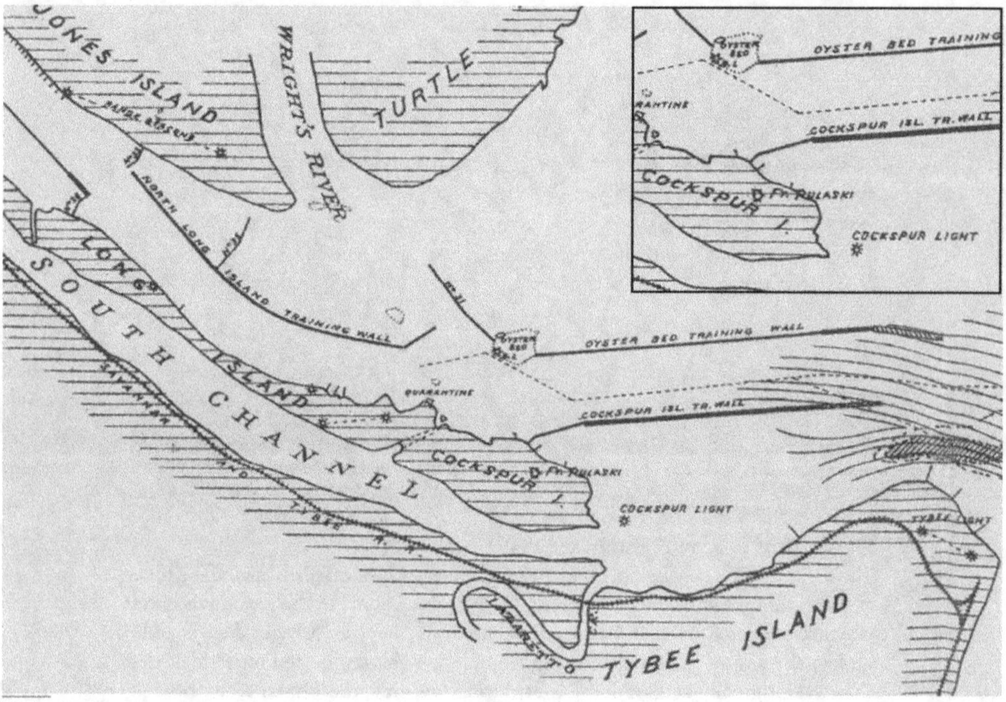

Tybee Roads c1894
This inset map from "*Map of the Entrance of Savannah Harbor, GA.*" prepared by the U.S. Corp. of Engineers clearly defines the approaches to the North and South Channels of the Savannah River and indicates the locations of the Cockspur and Oyster Beds Lighthouses. Oyster Bed Island – which originated as a 1-acre oyster shoal, is located at the eastern tip of the Tybee National Wildlife Refuge which today forms the north shore of the river. Jones and Oyster Bed Islands are now connected as a result of decades of dredge spoil deposits by the Corp. of Engineers.

The first Cockspur Lighthouse was destroyed by a hurricane, which was communicated in September of 1854 in two letters from H. Roberts – then the Superintendent of the Lights for the Savannah Area, to the Lighthouse Board (formerly the Lighthouse Service). After several months of inaction, Captain Jeremy F. Gilmer – the new Superintending Engineer of Lighthouses on the Savannah River, sent estimates and requested funds for the reconstruction of the tower as well as improvements to the keeper's cottage, which apparently survived the storm.[8] The 1855 Annual Report of the Lighthouse Board detailed the appropriation for the new lighthouse:

> *The beacon-light for the South Channel of the Savannah River is to be rebuilt on the same foundation and enlarged. The cost will be about $6,000. A brick foundation should be built under the keeper's house on Cockspur Island to make it more comfortable in winter, and a small frame kitchen added. These additions can be made for $450.*

At Gilmer's request, the ironwork for the new beacon – "the lantern housing, lantern level floor, vents, lantern door and door frame," was manufactured in Baltimore.[9] The bricks used in the construction of the lighthouse - Savannah Grey bricks, are the same type that were manufactured locally by enslaved labor at the Hermitage Plantation in Savanah – the same brick used in the construction of Fort Pulaski. A sixth order Fresnel lens was installed in place of the oil lamp with which the earlier tower was equipped.[10]

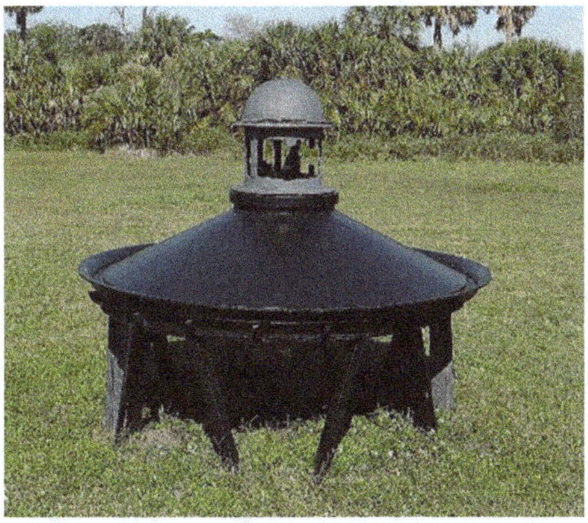

Original Cupola – Cockspur Island Lighthouse c2024

At left is the original cupola that was a part of the ironwork forged in Baltimore for the construction of the Cockspur Island Lighthouse as requested by Captain Gilmer in 1855. The original cupola – on display near the entrance to the Lighthouse Overlook Trail at Fort Pulaski, was replaced by a replica in 2000 as it was deemed beyond repair – it was determined that the replica would better protect the interior of the masonry tower and its remaining original iron components. *Photograph courtesy of the author.*

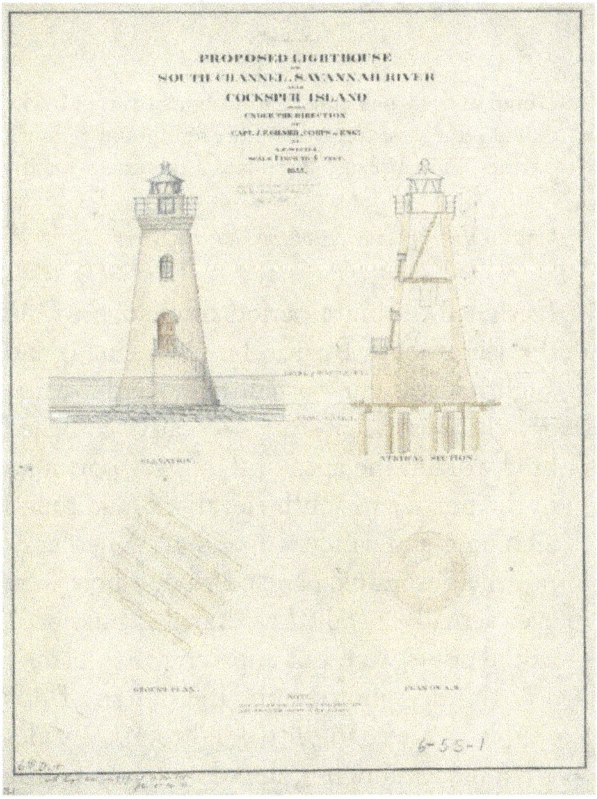

"Proposed Lighthouse for the South Channel, Savannah River Near Cockspur Island" – c1855

The drawings at left are the earliest images of the Cockspur Island Lighthouse. An earlier drawing attributed to 6th Lighthouse District Engineer Capt. Jeremy F. Gilmer of the Corps of Engineers reveals plans for a different looking, slightly taller beacon with a larger, more elaborate lantern room. Housed in the National Archives, the proposed plans feature the following handwritten comments dated December 4, 1855: *"Approved with the modifications recommended in report of Corps of Engineers of 30 Nov. 1855"*. The final plans (at left) were drawn by A.P. Wetter "under the direction of Capt. J.F. Gilmer, Corp of Engineers." This plan also features a handwritten note: *"Design as modified in accordance with the instructions of the Board of Dec. 4th 1855." Drawing courtesy of the National Archives.*

Detail View of a Vertical Section of the Cockspur Lighthouse – c1855 At left – a drawing showing a cross section of the interior of the lighthouse from a "Proposed Lighthouse for the South Channel, Savannah River near Cockspur Island."

Completed in 1856, the Cockspur Island lighthouse is a conical brick tower with a base that is 16 feet in diameter, is 46 feet tall, and features three levels – the first being 8 feet above sea level as the tidal islet it is situated on is underwater at high tide. A spiral brick staircase leads to the first landing, which is constructed of wood. A wooden ladder provides access to an iron hatch in the lantern room floor. The lantern room is encircled by an exterior catwalk with an iron guardrail, which is accessed via a small iron door.[11] Round arch wood windows provide natural light at each landing.

Detail of the Cockspur Island Lighthouse – c1855 At left – the west elevation of the lighthouse as drawn on the original plans, "Proposed Lighthouse for the South Channel, Savannah River near Cockspur Island." *Drawing courtesy of the National Archives.*

Designed during a period of change within the Lighthouse Board, the Cockspur Island Lighthouse is fairly ornate compared to earlier lighthouses, featuring decorative corbelled brickwork at the apex of the tower, portholes in the north and south elevations, and round arch door and window openings. Whether or not the decorative paneled wood doors were ever actually installed as drawn is unknown, as the doors were not apparent on a historic 19th century photograph. The design of this simple yet elegant little lighthouse exudes a sophistication not found in most of the

Cockspur Island Lighthouse c2021
Photograph courtesy of the National Park Service

lighthouses which came before it, perhaps as a result of being designed by the highly trained engineers of the U.S. Army Corps of Engineers.

The iron lantern at the top of the tower features 10 trapezoidal glass panes. The original configuration of the windows is unknown – the round arch wooden fanlights and fixed nine-light windows that are in place today represent a historical approximation. A unique aspect of the towers design can be seen in its base, which was designed as a "bow" facing the river to calm incoming waves. A Historic American Buildings Survey report completed in 1980 suggests that the bow utilized in the Cockspur Lighthouse is a precursor to a "later design feature utilized in wave-swept (off-shore) towers."[12]

Most histories attribute the design of the Cockspur Lighthouse to engineers of the 6th District, Corp. of Engineers. The lighthouse's design represents an early departure from the old "early federal period" lighthouses associated with the Winslow Lewis-era. In 1852, the authority to oversee the construction, repair, and maintenance of lighthouses in the United States was moved from the Lighthouse Establishment to the Lighthouse Board, which delegated the supervision and construction of aids to navigation to the U.S. Army Corp. of Engineers.[13] By 1857 the Lighthouse Board adopted a standardized plan for lighthouse construction.[14] While the basis for this standardized plan is not clear at this time, it is worth noting that the initial design for the Cockspur Island Lighthouse – designed by Captain Jeremy F. Gilmer in November 1855, bears several similar characteristics.

Jeremy Francis Gilmer graduated from West Point in 1839, serving briefly as an Assistant Professor in Engineering at the Military Academy. He spent most of his career with the Army Corp. of Engineers engaged in the repair and construction of fortifications. In 1848 he was appointed Superintending Engineer of repairs of Fort Pulaski and Fort Jackson and of the improvement of the Savannah River – a post he held until 1858. During this time, Gilmer also served as Superintending Engineer of Lighthouses on the Savannah River from 1855 – 1857, when he designed and oversaw the construction of the Cockspur Island Lighthouse.[15] *Photograph Courtesy of William Bjornstad*

Detail of the First Design for the Cockspur Island Lighthouse – c1855
At right – the west elevation of the lighthouse as drawn on the unrealized first draft plans, entitled "Proposed Lighthouse for South Channel, Savannah River near Cockspur Island, by J.F. Gilmer, Corp. of Engineers." The design for the lantern room – which was completely revised in the final approved plans, is practically identical to the lantern room depicted on the standardized lighthouse plans that would later be adopted by the Lighthouse Board in 1856-57. (see Chapter 4 for an expanded discussion of lighthouse types and the "standardized lighthouse plan.") *Drawing courtesy of the National Archives*

Cockspur Island Lighthouse – *Photograph courtesy of the National Park Service*

While much is known about the history of the Cockspur Island Lighthouse, the question of who built the beacon – the masons, carpenters, laborers, remains unanswered at the time of this writing. Clearly, skilled brick masons were employed in the construction of the sturdy little lighthouse since it has weathered both the tides and powerful storms during the last 169 years. Records confirm that the bricks used in its construction are Savannah Greys manufactured by enslaved Africans at the Hermitage Plantation – so this contribution has been documented. While the specific individuals who were involved in the construction of the lighthouse remain unknown, it is entirely possible that enslaved craftsman and/or laborers from local plantations participated in its construction, as was the case in the construction of Fort Pulaski during the 1830s and 1840s.

Advertisement – Daily Georgian, 1836

The Corp. of Engineers placed multiple ads like this one in Savannah papers soliciting the lease of enslaved workers from local plantation owners during the construction of Fort Pulaski. It is possible that the Corp. of Engineers employed a similar arrangement in the construction of the Cockspur Island Lighthouse. Skilled enslaved craftsmen are known to have lived and worked at Fort Pulaski as late as 1861. Thomas Franklin – an enslaved bricklayer who was working at the fort, left Fort Pulaski before the blockade, making his way to Tybee Island and freedom behind Union lines.[16]

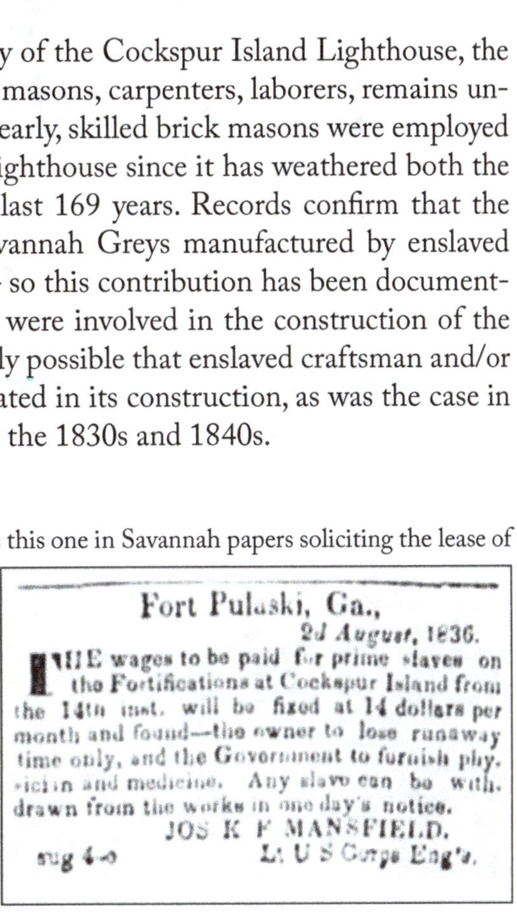

Fort Pulaski, Ga.,

2d August, 1836.

THE wages to be paid for prime slaves on the Fortifications at Cockspur Island from the 14th inst. will be fixed at 14 dollars per month and found—the owner to lose runaway time only, and the Government to furnish physician and medicine. Any slave can be withdrawn from the works in one day's notice.

JOS K F MANSFIELD,

aug 4-o Lt U S Corps Eng's.

Georgia's Island Lighthouses, Sketch by Robert Klein

Chapter Three

Georgia's Lighthouses

The developmental history of lighthouses and aids to navigation in the United States can easily be traced locally by studying the growth and development of the port of Savannah during the 18th and subsequent centuries and the growing significance of other ports along the coast of Georgia through the 19th and early 20th centuries. As stated in the Report of the Lighthouse Board in 1855,

> *"... the lighthouse system of the United States has grown up from small beginnings – only eight lights in 1789, to fifty-five in 1820 – to its present enlarged condition of three-hundred and eighty-one lights in 1851".*

At the time of this report, there were nine brick lighthouses on the Georgia coast.[1] With advances in technology, improvements in aids to navigation led to the development of more economical and mobile beacons, range lights, and other devices, with the eventual abandonment of the traditional masonry lighthouse as an option for new beacons by the early 20th century. Although only five traditional masonry lighthouses remain standing, all eras and classes of lighthouses that make up the U.S. lighthouse system are represented along the Georgia coast.

Colonial (1764 – 1791) and Early Federal (1792 – 1817)

The earliest lighthouses in the United States were built by local craftsman utilizing locally-available materials. Colonial towers were octagonal in design and featured solid masonry walls that were many feet thick at the base.[2]

Colonial lighthouses were followed by a class of lighthouses constructed during the New Republic period – referred to as "Early Federal Octagonals" by historian Russ Rowlett of the University of North Carolina at Chapel Hill. One of the first acts of the first Congress when it met in 1789 was to take control of the new nation's lighthouses and aids to navigation. During this period, new lighthouses were authorized by Congress and officials at the highest levels of the federal government were involved in their construction. Early federal lighthouses (1792 – 1817) were generally taller than colonial lights, were better engineered, were adequately funded, and were carefully built by skilled, experienced craftsmen.

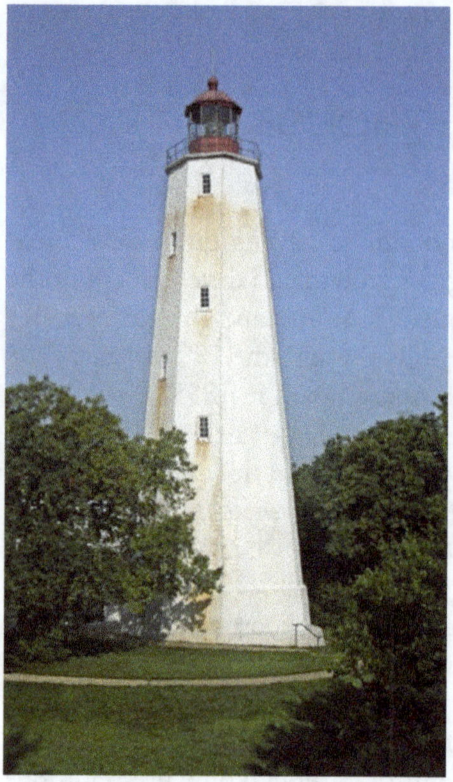

Sandy Hook Lighthouse, New Jersey c1764
The 85 feet tall lighthouse at Sandy Hook is the oldest lighthouse in the nation and one of a handful of colonial lighthouses still standing. Its successful octagonal design served as the basis for two other colonial lighthouses – Cape Henlopen (c1765) in Delaware and **Tybee Island (c1773)** in Georgia (below in a photo dating to 1863).[3] *Photographs courtesy Kraig Anderson and the National Archives*

The early federal class of lighthouses are characterized as being "blunt, massive towers with solid walls, very thick at the base and tapering like pyramids." Almost all early federal towers feature the same octagonal design, which is based on the design of the successful colonial lighthouse at Sandy Hook (c1764), New Jersey.[4]

Built in 1773, the 90-feet tall Tybee Island Lighthouse was the only brick lighthouse of its class built in Georgia during the Colonial Period. In 1791 it was lit for the first time with spermaceti candles (having been an unattended daymark before that time).[5] The first St. Simons Lighthouse – built in 1810, was the sole example of the Early Federal class of lighthouses built in the state. It was replaced by the second St. Simons Lighthouse in 1872.[6]

New London Harbor, Connecticut c1801
The 89 feet tall lighthouse at New London Harbor is comparable in height and design to the first St. Simons Lighthouse, built in 1810. Pictured in 1845 (above, right), the original St. Simons Lighthouse was 85 feet tall and was one of eleven early federal towers to utilize the octagonal design inspired by the Sandy Hook Lighthouse. Nine of these towers are still standing with five remaining in service.[7] *Photographs courtesy of Cody Chase, SAH Archipedia and the National Archives.*

Antebellum/Lighthouse Establishment (1820-1852)

The class of lighthouses built during the nation's antebellum period are closely associated with its most prolific builder – Winslow Lewis, and the bureaucrat who served as the Fifth Auditor of the Treasury – Stephen Pleasonton.

Lewis was a former sea captain who developed a lighting apparatus to illuminate lighthouses. In 1812, Congress bought the patent rights for Lewis's lighting system and contracted with him to equip all the nation's lighthouses. In 1816 Lewis was again awarded a contract by Congress, this time to supply oil to all the nation's light stations and to make annual inspections to ensure that they were being operated properly.[8]

In 1820, the Secretary of the Treasury appointed Stephen Pleasonton superintendent of U.S. lighthouses – a post he would serve until 1852. Although he had no knowledge of engineering or construction, one of his duties was to award contracts for the maintenance and construction of lighthouses. As an auditor of the Treasury Department, Pleasonton's principal concern was the economical administration of the Lighthouse Establishment and keeping costs as low as possible. Because Lewis was almost always the lowest bidder – and was likely known to Pleasanton from his earlier work, most of the lighthouses built during this time were constructed by him.[9]

Sapelo Island Lighthouse (c1820) and Keepers Cottage, McIntosh County, GA. – photographed in the late 19th Century.
The 65-feet tall Sapelo Island Lighthouse was among Winslow Lewis's first commissions – along with the Cumberland Island Lighthouse (GA), which was built in the same year. By the time this photograph was taken, the beacons distinctive "bird cage" lantern room had been replaced with a new one because of damage it had suffered during the Civil War.[10] In addition to the war, the transition from the Lighthouse Establishment to the Lighthouse Board also brought a nationwide modernization of U.S. lighthouses as the federal government adopted the more reliable Fresnel lens, which often necessitated the installation of a new lantern room housing.[11] As a result, very few of the Lewis-designed "bird cage" lantern rooms have survived. *Photograph courtesy of the National Archives.*

As a result of his virtual monopoly on lighthouse construction, Lewis drew a standardized design to meet demand. He developed a simple design for a conical brick tower that varied in height from 25 feet to 65 feet. His short, squat towers also featured a distinctive "bird cage" lantern that housed his patented Lewis lamps.[12]

Little Cumberland Island Lighthouse (c1838) Although built by John Hastings of Boston, the 61-feet tall Little Cumberland Island Lighthouse was equipped with a Lewis lighting apparatus due to his unique relationship with the Lighthouse Establishment. As a result, the lighthouse bears the distinctive bird cage lantern room associated with lighthouses of the antebellum class.[13] *Photographs courtesy of the U.S. Coast Guard (left) and Lighthouse Friends (below).*

Five brick beacons from this class of lighthouses were built in Georgia during this time: Great Cumberland Island and Sapelo Island in 1820 (both by Lewis); Wolf Island in 1822; Little Cumberland Island in 1838; and the first Cockspur Island Lighthouse in 1849. The beacons at Sapelo and Little Cumberland Islands are the only ones that remain standing (the Great Cumberland Island Lighthouse was moved to Amelia Island in 1838).[14]

First Cockspur Island Lighthouse c1849 As drawn by Savannah/New York architect John S. Norris, the first Cockspur Island Lighthouse bears all the hallmarks of the antebellum class of lighthouses built under the direct and indirect influence of prolific lighthouse contractor Winslow Lewis. Lewis's standard design for lighthouses came in 5 different heights – 25, 30, 40, 50, and 65 feet.[15] While the designer of the first Cockspur light is unknown, its 25-foot height, squat, tapered shape, and bird cage lantern room suggest Lewis as a strong possibility. *Drawing courtesy of the National Archives.*

Sapelo Island Lighthouse c1820
The Sapelo Island Lighthouse in McIntosh County is the oldest unaltered lighthouse in Georgia. It is also the oldest remaining lighthouse in the nation built by Winslow Lewis and is among his earliest commissions. Although Lewis is known to have been responsible for the construction of at least eighty lighthouses – and likely several more, very few of his commissions survive today as a result of several factors: many were poorly sited, leading to their destruction by erosion or storms; inferior construction techniques were often used to cut costs, making the beacons unstable; most were replaced during the 1850s because they were too short to be effective.[16] Only eleven lighthouses of the Lewis-Pleasonton class remain standing – with most of these being among the taller iterations of his standardized plan.[17] The Sapelo Island Lighthouse was restored to its 1890 appearance and relit in 1998.[18] *Photograph courtesy of Kraig Anderson/Lighthouse Friends.*

Lighthouse Board/Reconstruction (1852 – 1869)

The class of lighthouses built after the mid-19th century were designed and constructed during a period of modernization orchestrated by the newly-authorized Lighthouse Board, which succeeded the Lighthouse Establishment in 1852. According to Russ Rowlett of the University of North Carolina at Chapel Hill, the lighthouses constructed during the Lewis-Pleasanton era had become - by this time, "embarrassingly inadequate and obsolete" by European standards. Mariners complained that the lighthouses were "too short, too dim, poorly located, or often out of service altogether."[19]

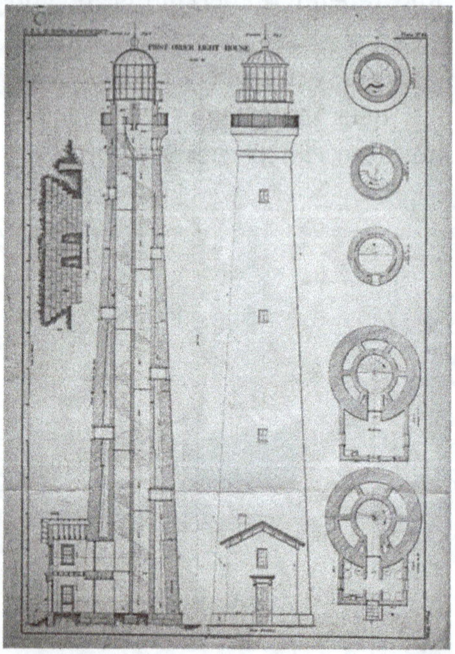

In 1847, Congress initially addressed this problem by directing that six proposed lighthouses be designed and built by military engineers instead of contractors selected by Pleasonton. In 1852, Congress made this arrangement permanent when it transferred responsibility for the nation's lighthouses to the Lighthouse Board, which was dominated by military officers.[20] Moving forward, lighthouses were designed by the chief engineer of each district, who also oversaw all aspects of construction. As a result, these designs often reflected the tastes and preferences of their designers. During the mid-1850s, the Lighthouse Board began developing a standard lighthouse plan for a tall brick tower (previous page, bottom right), which they adopted c1856-57. The plan called for double walls, an iron staircase around a central column, a brick apron that flares out at the apex to support the gallery deck, and a gable roof oil house/work room that serves as an entry foyer to the beacon. A railed gallery deck and a distinct lantern room with domed cupola were also characteristic elements of the standardized lighthouse plan.[21]

Cape Romain Light Station, SC c1893
This historic photo of the Sixth District light station at Cape Romain, South Carolina illustrates the difference between the old antebellum style towers and the modern tall towers that began to replace them during the 1850s and 1860s. The short, blunt tower on the left is a 65-foot model built by Winslow Lewis in 1827 – the 154-feet tall tower on the right is a first-order lighthouse built in 1858.[22] Aside from its octagonal shape, the modern brick lighthouse on the right exhibits most of the key characteristics of the Lighthouse Board's standard plan. *Photograph courtesy of the National Archives.*

Two brick beacons from this class of lighthouses were built in Georgia during this time: a first-order lighthouse at Tybee Island in 1867; and a third-order lighthouse at St. Simons Island in 1872. Both lighthouses were built – or in the case of the Tybee Island Lighthouse – rebuilt, as a result of events that occurred during the American Civil War. Many lighthouses in the South were either damaged or destroyed to prevent their military use by the opposing side.[23]

Tybee Island Lighthouse c1773/1867
The rebuilt Tybee Island Lighthouse in a historic Photograph taken c1881 (above). In 1861, a Confederate raiding party set fire to the then 100-foot tower, destroying the lantern and the interior wooden staircase. After the war, engineers reduced the original tower to 60 feet and then extended it to its present height of 154 feet from the ground to the top of the ventilator ball. The new tower retains an octagonal shape but a noticeable difference in the taper of the tower can be seen 60 feet from ground level where the new tower extends out of the old base.[24] The Tybee lighthouse was clearly rebuilt utilizing the Lighthouse Board's standardized lighthouse plan for first-order lighthouses as it exhibits all its hallmarks. Had the lower 60 feet of the octagonal colonial period tower not been reused in its reconstruction, the new tower would have been conical in shape. *Photograph courtesy of the National Archives.*

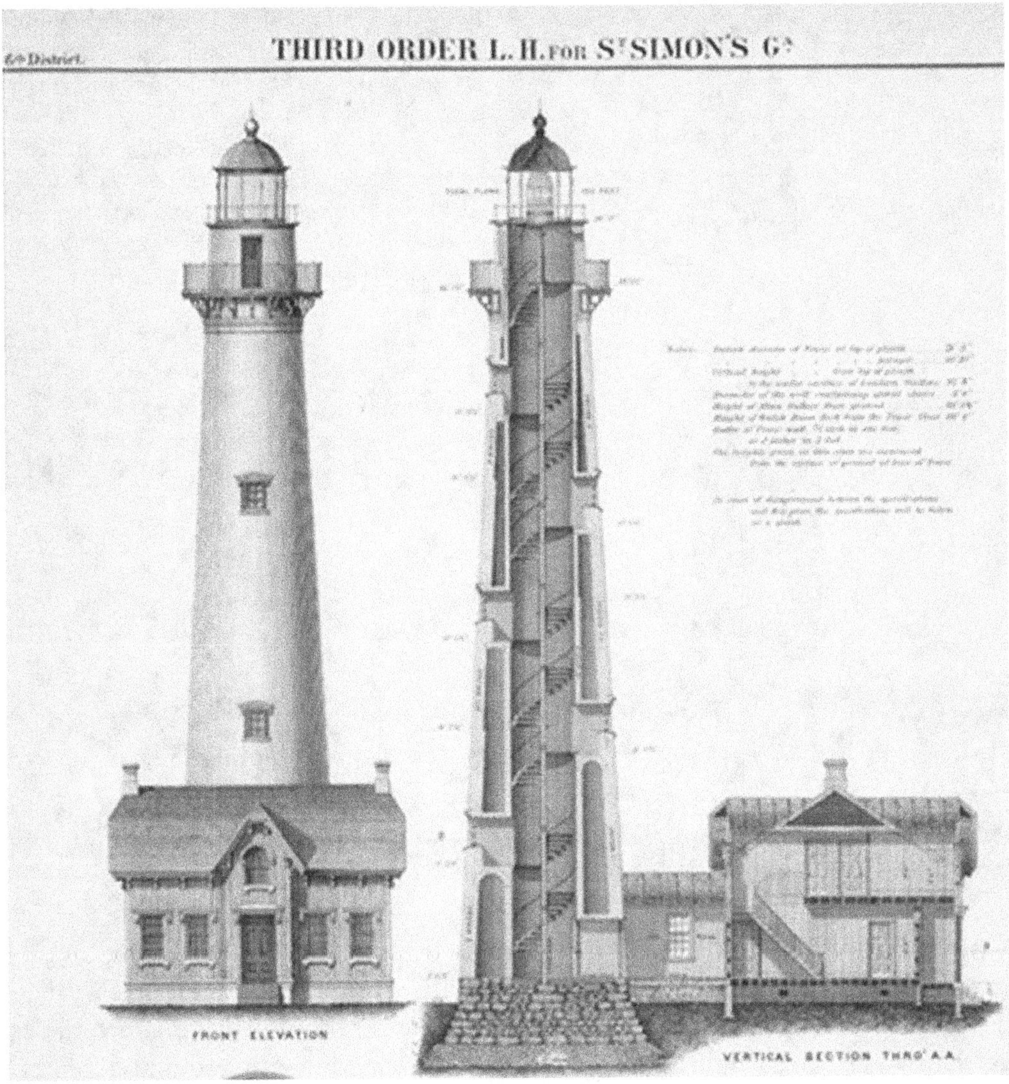

St. Simons Island Lighthouse c1872

This lighthouse was designed in 1867 by prolific Savannah architect Charles Clusky – it is the only example of this class of lighthouse in Georgia that exemplifies all the elements of the standardized lighthouse plan. However, it too displays some deviations that can be attributed to its architect – such as its Victorian-era detailing (decorative window molds on the lighthouse) and its highly ornate Italianate style keeper's cottage. At the time of its construction, there was no standard plan for keeper's cottages, which appears to have been left to the creativity of the engineers in charge. Like the Tybee Island Lighthouse, civilian engineers/architects under the employ and supervision of Lighthouse District engineers were utilized in the rebuilding of both lighthouses because so many were damaged or destroyed during the Civil War.[25] *Drawing courtesy of the National Archives.*

Georgia's Postbellum "Tall Towers"
Both the Tybee and St. Simons lighthouses are examples of the standardization and modernization of the U.S. Lighthouse Service that occurred during the decades following the authorization of the Lighthouse Board in 1852. By the 1880s, this standardization was extended to the keeper's cottages and other aspects of the lighthouse service. *Photographs courtesy of the author and the National Archives.*

A third brick lighthouse was built in Georgia during this period – the Sixth-Order Cockspur Island Lighthouse. At 46 feet tall, this beacon cannot be classified as a "tall tower." In addition to height, it also lacks several of the characteristics of the "standardized lighthouse plan," such as cast-iron stairs around a central column, a gable roofed oil room at its base, and the standard large, multi-light lantern room with domed cupola. It does, however, reflect some of the early thinking of the period, having a flared brick apron at the apex to support the gallery deck as well as a gallery railing – two characteristics that would later become part of the Lighthouse Board's standard plan. Designed in 1855, the Cockspur Island Lighthouse is representative of the evolution in lighthouse design that was occurring at the time and is emblematic of the early transition from the old antebellum-period lighthouses to the modern, standardized lighthouses designed by district engineers during the Lighthouse Board era.

Cockspur Island Lighthouse – c2020
Photograph courtesy of the Friends of Cockspur Island Lighthouse

It should be noted that the site of the Cockspur Island Lighthouse – on a wave-swept islet, and its purpose as a channel beacon to guide ships at the mouth of the Savannah River, was certainly a deciding factor in determining its height as well as its design. A tall tower of the first or second order would not be necessary (or possible) for this site and its purpose. Unlike a first-order lighthouse – which would be sited inland from the shore and would need to be tall with a bright light so ocean-going vessels could see it from great distances while at sea, river channel and harbor lights do not require great heights and only need a focal visibility sufficient to guide vessels along treacherous approaches.

View northwest of Cockspur Island and the Cockspur Lighthouse
Photograph courtesy of Allen Lewis

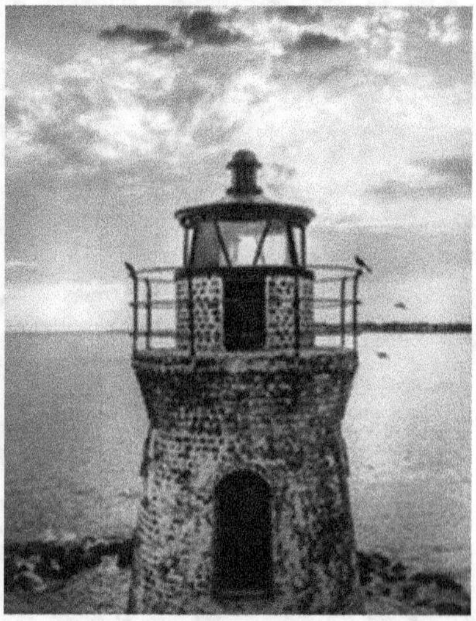

Portland Breakwater Lighthouse – Portland, Maine
Pictured in a historic photo just after its construction (far left), the Sixth-Order Portland Breakwater Lighthouse was a "minor light" built to assist mariners in navigating the "shoal-laced approach to the harbor at Portland, Maine." America's earliest lighthouses were built to mark the entrances to ports – like the Tybee Island Lighthouse at the mouth of the Savannah River. As articulated by Wayne Wheeler in his article "The Portland Breakwater Light Station," after these primary lights were established, "*... additional aids to navigation were constructed to better define harbors. They included small post lights, buoys, and lesser light stations.*"[26] The Cockspur Island and Oyster Beds Beacon Light Station was one such "minor light station" built to improve navigation along the Savannah River corridor. The Cockspur Lighthouse (above right) and the Portland Breakwater Lighthouse were built a year apart and feature identical cast iron canopies as well as gallery railings, making it apparent that standardization of lighthouse design at all levels was a priority for the Lighthouse Board soon after it was established. As both lights feature similar-sized lantern rooms and were equipped with less powerful Fresnel lens, it appears that this smaller canopy was intended as the standard design for channel and harbor lights of the sixth order. *Photographs courtesy of the U.S. Coast Guard and Frank Logue (left to right, respectively).*

Chapter Four

THE LIGHT STATION

Photograph courtesy of the Friends of Cockspur Island Lighthouse

Constructed between 1837 and 1839, the Cockspur Island and Oyster Beds Beacons were the first of a series of small daymarks, beacons, and range lights that were built during the mid- to late-19th century to improve navigation along the Savannah River corridor. After the beacons were converted into lighthouses in 1849, the Cockspur Island and Oyster Beds Beacon Lighthouses became part of a true "light station" as a keeper would be necessary for the first time to maintain the beacons and to keep them lit. As part of the work accomplished in establishing the light station, a "suitable Keeper's House" was built on Cockspur Island for the lighthouse keeper and his family. At the time, the Cockspur Island and Oyster Beds Beacon Light Station and the Tybee Island Light Station were the principal aids to navigation for Tybee Roads and the entrance to the Savannah River. Also known as the South and North Channel lights, respectively, the beacons were built two miles west of the Tybee Lighthouse and were intended to guide ships up the Savannah River, past Tybee Island, and around Cockspur and Elba Islands.

The first three keepers assigned to the light station were John H. Lightburn (1849), James Callan (1850), and Cornelius Maher (1851-1853). The first keepers of the light station were responsible for both lighthouses, making multiple trips daily to the beacons to service the lights.[1] While the islet in which the Cockspur Lighthouse was located could be reached by foot at low tide, the Oyster Beds Beacon was located on a small island in the North Channel and could only be reached by boat, which made it highly dangerous to reach at high tide. In February of 1853, the boat Cornelius Maher was rowing to the Oyster Beds Beacon capsized, and he drowned. Cornelius' widow – Mary Maher, took over as lighthouse keeper, becoming one of the few female keepers employed by the Lighthouse Board along the Savannah River.[2] In 1854 the original Cockspur Lighthouse was destroyed by a gale.[3] Mary continued to serve as keeper of the light station through 1856, maintaining and servicing the Oyster Beds Beacon.[4]

In 1855 Capt. Jeremy F. Gilmer became the new Superintending Engineer of Lighthouses for the Savannah River.[5] In addition to designing and supervising the construction of the new Cockspur Island Lighthouse, Gilmer made several improvements to the navigational system along the Savannah River. He outlined these improvements in his report to the Lighthouse Board in 1855:

> *"Since resuming the charge of the works of this city, I have built three day beacons – two on Elba Island, Savannah river, and on the northern bank of the river – as marks for vessels when passing over the "Horse-shoe" and "Pumpkin" Bank, and made extensive repairs to the light-house on the eastern end of Fig Island . . ."*[6]

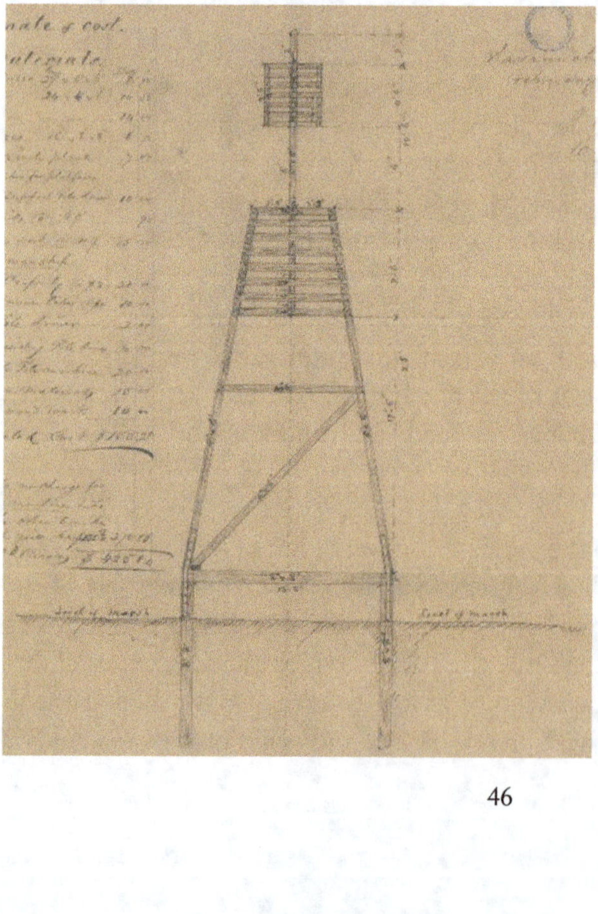

"Proposed Plan for Three Beacons to indicate the best Channels over the Horse Shoe & Pumpkin banks, in the Savannah River, Ga" February 25, 1855
Gilmer submitted this proposal to his Sixth District superiors in the Winter of 1855. As indicated by the drawing at left, each of the proposed "beacons" would be twenty-five feet tall and of frame construction – the total cost of the project was estimated at $425.86. Day markers such as these were inexpensive, easy to construct, and were often a temporary way of providing adequate navigational aids when dealing with limited resources. As was the case with the Cockspur Lighthouse, these wooden markers were often a precursor to a more permanent and substantial beacon. *Drawing courtesy of the National Archives.*

By this time a third lighthouse had been added to the Savannah River navigational system. The Fig Island Lighthouse (c1850) – a small wooden harbor light mounted on the top of a keeper's dwelling, was located on the north side of the river about ½ mile east of the city wharfs.[7] The light station was severely damaged by the same gale that destroyed the original Cockspur Lighthouse.[8]

After the completion of the present Cockspur Lighthouse in 1856, Thomas Quinliven (1856) briefly served as the fifth keeper of the lights followed by the long tenure of the sixth keeper, Patrick Egan (1856-1867). By this time the light station was assigned an assistant lighthouse keeper – James Cullen, who served from 1857-1859.[9]

Patrick Egan's first stint as the head keeper of the Cockspur and Oyster Beds Beacon Lighthouses was interrupted by the events of the Civil War. After Union troops took control of Tybee Island in 1861, the lights were extinguished. On April 10, 1862, Union batteries on Tybee Island began the bombardment of the Fort, which continued throughout the following day. Despite being in the direct line of fire, the Cockspur Island Lighthouse remained unscathed.[10]

"The War in Georgia – The Bombardment of Fort Pulaski – Second Day Friday, April 11, 1862"
This illustration from *Frank Leslie's Illustrated Newspaper* depicts the Cockspur Island Lighthouse on the left at low tide as the shells from the Union batteries on Tybee fly overhead. This southwest view appears to be from the perspective of one of the Union ships moored in Tybee Roads.

As reported in the Savannah News Press, the lighthouse was unharmed because the angle required to send the shells the proper distance propelled them over the top of the beacon, rather than through it.[11] National news correspondents present at the scene provided illustrations which depict the lighthouse in the midst of battle, as well as in its aftermath.

"The War in Georgia – Surrender of Fort... From A Sketch by Our Special Artist, W.T. Crane" This illustration from *Frank Leslie's Illustrated Newspaper* depicts the Cockspur Island Lighthouse and Fort Pulaski from the perspective of the Union batteries on Tybee Island after its surrender.

Daymark Island c1863 – In a photo taken from the northwest corner of Fort Pulaski, one of several unlit brick beacons – or "daymarks," is barely discernable in the North Channel of the Savannah River. This beacon was likely intended to help guide ships safely to the fort's North Pier adjacent the Pulaski Beacon. *Photograph courtesy of the National Park Service.*

Arrangements to relight the beacons were begun shortly after the end of the War. In 1865, Inspector Powell of the Third Lighthouse District of New York responded to instructions from the Lighthouse Board to send a Sixth-Order Lens for the Cockspur Lighthouse. After making minor repairs – and painting the beacon white to serve as its daymark, the Cockspur Island Lighthouse was relit on April 25, 1866.[12] During this time, Patrick Egan continued to serve as head keeper with Joe Smith (1866-1867) serving as assistant keeper of the Cockspur and Oyster Beds Beacon Light Station.[13]

In 1867 Thomas F. Floyd (1867-1868) succeeded Egan as head keeper of the light station with Eagan's son – John (1867-1870), serving as assistant keeper. Floyd's tenure was short.

In 1868 Patrick Eagan (1868-1877) returned for a second long stint as head keeper of the light station with a succession of his sons serving as his first assistant. By 1870, Thomas Eagan (1870-1871) had replaced his older brother John as assistant lighthouse keeper.[14] In August of 1871, the two keepers – along with Michael Eagan, one of the juvenile sons, took the boat out during a heavy storm to service the Oyster Beds Beacon. Their boat capsized; Patrick and his younger son Michael managed to hang on to the overturned boat while Thomas was lost to the treacherous waters. His body was never located.[15] The Annual Report of the Lighthouse Board alludes to this tragic event years later in its assessment of the dangerous conditions at the light station:

> *"This light is attended by the same keepers who attend the Cockspur Beacon. During heavy northeast winds they run great risks in crossing the river to reach the light, and one keeper is known to have lost his life, and another is supposed to have shared the same fate in trying to reach the light. A dwelling on iron piles, adjacent the light, is recommended by both district officers, and its cost is estimated at $11,000."*[16]

Despite the loss of Head Lighthouse Keeper Cornelius Maher in 1853 and First Assistant Lighthouse Keeper Thomas Eagan in 1871, a separate keeper's dwelling adjacent the Oyster Beds Beacon – on Oyster Bed Island, was never built. Robert Egan (1871-1875) would replace his brother as assistant keeper following his death and was later followed by his brother John (1875-76) in 1875 during their father Patrick's final years as head keeper.[17]

In 1874 a gale severely damaged the Oyster Beds Beacon, as reported in the 1875 Annual Report of the Lighthouse Board:

"... the boat landing at this station was entirely destroyed, and the tower damaged by debris of the wharf being dashed against it, tearing out chunks of the masonry, and causing the tower to be cracked from top to bottom. The landing has been rebuilt, and the brick work repaired; and it is proposed to place a talus of rip-rap around the base as an addition protection. The cost of these repairs was paid from the general appropriations for repairs of light-houses."[18]

The recommendations to place a "talus of rip-rap around the base" of the Oyster Beds Beacon went unheeded, and by 1879, district engineers reported that high tides had washed away the soil from the foundation of the brick tower, exposing its lower courses.[19] A second request for the placing of rip-rap would go unanswered until 1886.[20]

Cockspur Island Lighthouse c1863 – In a photo taken from the southeast corner of Fort Pulaski following its capture by Union Forces, the Cockspur Lighthouse is visible to the east in the South Channel of the Savannah River. *Photograph courtesy of the National Park Service*

Throughout the 1870s district officials continuously recommended the construction of a new keeper's quarters for the Cockspur and Oyster Beds Beacon Light Station. In 1874, district engineers wrote the following to be included in the Annual Report:

"The beacon is a substantial brick structure, resting on a foundation of piles. The keeper's dwelling, built in 1855, is a small one-story frame structure resting on piles. The building and piles are so thoroughly rotten that further repairs would be a waste of money. An appropriation of $10,000 is therefore recommended to rebuild the structure."[21]

After reporting in 1876 that the Cockspur Lighthouse had been "*fitted with storm doors for the lantern, and the stairs and landing repaired,*" district officials tried a second time to obtain the funds to erect a new dwelling for the light station:

> "*The keeper's dwelling ... is more than twenty years old, and so decayed that further repairs are unadvisable. It is also so near the ground that during severe gales the water rises above the floor. This dwelling accommodates the keepers of both the Oyster Beds and Cockspur beacons. An appropriation of $7,000 is recommended to build a suitable dwelling.*"[22]

By 1878, district officials were recommending new keeper's dwellings be built for each lighthouse. After reporting that both towers were whitewashed, repaired, and the woodwork repainted, it was revealed that the dilapidated keeper's house had been struck by lightning and was now almost uninhabitable. District officers recommended the building of new keepers' dwellings adjacent each tower, acknowledging that it would be costly as each would have to be built on iron piles. The estimated cost for the new Cockspur keeper's quarters was $10,000 and for the Oyster Beds Beacon, $11,000.[23] These appropriations were never made.

Tybee Island Range Front Light c1877
The Lighthouse Board made several efforts throughout the late 19th Century to improve navigation along the Savannah River, constructing additional beacons and day markers as well as minor light houses. In 1867 the first of a series of "range lights" were introduced when a frame, skeletal tower equipped with a Fourth-Order Fresnel lens was built east of the Tybee Lighthouse, providing a "range" for mariners entering the Savannah River. Range lights are a pair of lights that are aligned to enable seamen to maintain the center of a channel. In 1877 the earlier range light was replaced by the more permanent iron beacon pictured at left.[24] By the end of the 1880s, several additional "ranges" had been established along the length of the river channel. *Photograph courtesy of the National Archives.*

By the late 1870s a fifth light station had been added along the Savannah River corridor. As early as 1870, appropriations for a new lighthouse to replace the Tybee Knoll Lightship No. 21 had been requested by district officials. In 1877 the Annual Report of the Lighthouse Board indicated that two five-acre tracts of land on the easterly end of Long Island (located in the Savannah River immediately west of Cockspur Island) had been acquired as sites for "*two range beacons to be built to mark the dredged cut through Tybee Knoll.*" In 1878 the Annual Report informed that "*...the structures for the front and rear lights have been built and an earthen causeway constructed from the landing to the front light, and thence to the rear light.*" The beacons of the Tybee Knoll Cut Range Light Station were each equipped with a sixth-order Fresnel lens and was lighted on November 1, 1879.[25]

By the end of the 1870s Patrick Eagan had been replaced by Charles W. Poland (1877-1881) as head keeper with George W. Martus (1877-1881) serving as assistant lighthouse keeper.[26] Martus (1881-1884) – the older brother of Florence, Savannah's "Waving Girl," had become head keeper by the time of the devastating hurricane that struck Tybee Island on August 27, 1881.

Tybee Knoll Cut Range Front and Rear Lighthouses, Long Island c1879
Designed in 1877 and built in 1878, these beacons were the second in a series of range lights established for "general river navigation" on the Savannah River. The front light – seen in the historic Photograph at left, faced the North Channel. The beacon is mounted on top of the keeper's cottage with the light emanating from the gable. Depicted in the drawing at left, the rear light faced the South Channel and was of frame construction. Both featured Eastlake style ornamentation – a design characteristic that was standard for lighthouse keeper's dwellings built by the Lighthouse Board during the 1870s and 1880s. *Photograph courtesy of the U.S. Coast Guard, drawing courtesy of the National Archives.*

Martus and assistant lighthouse keeper James Feeley (1881-1884) took refuge in the casements of Fort Pulaski, where it was reported that the water rose to five feet over the parade ground. During the storm, the water rose halfway up the Cockspur Lighthouse, and all of Cockspur Island was submerged, resulting in the destruction of the old keeper's cottage.[27] The recently-completed Tybee Knoll Cut Range Light Station on Long Island was also severely damaged by the hurricane, which destroyed the rear tower.[28]

Tybee Knoll Cut Range Light Station – Front Light Boat Landing, photo c1915
One of two boat landings with an "elevated plank walk" that connected each light to the keeper's cottage. As indicated in annual reports throughout the late 19th and early 20th centuries, Sixth District officials were constantly rebuilding the wharfs and plank walks associated with the light stations along the Savannah River, whether due to damage from frequent storms or from changes in the course of the river. *Photograph courtesy of the National Archives.*

In 1881, an appropriation of $60,000 was made to "*light the Savannah River between its mouth and the city of Savannah.*" As indicated in the Annual Reports of the Lighthouse Board:

> *"It is proposed to erect "twelve iron lighthouses, two on Daufuskie, near Bloody Point, three on Jones Island, two on Elba Island, and two near Fort Jackson. The metal work for these structures is completed and ready for the erection at the sites."*

Referred to in the Annual Reports of the Lighthouse Board as the "Savannah River Lights," these twelve light houses made up six light stations, each consisting of two range lights complete with a keeper's dwelling, wharfs, and boat houses.[29] These new light stations completed the ranges begun at Tybee Island in 1867 and more recently on Long Island with the Tybee Knoll Cut Range Lights.

The 1881 Annual Report also shows that district officials recommended the discontinuation of the Oyster Beds Beacon upon the completion of the new river lights. The perceived obsolescence of the lighthouse may explain the Lighthouse

Board's reluctance to appropriate funds for a new keeper's dwelling during the prior decade, in addition to its need to allocate its limited resources to the completion of its ambitious new project to complete the Savannah River Lights. Instead of replacing the keeper's cottage destroyed by the hurricane of 1881, the keepers of the Cockspur and Oyster Beds Beacons were housed in temporary quarters within Fort Pulaski.[30]

As reported in the Annual Report of the Lighthouse Board, all the iron beacons that made up the new system of river lights were in place and first "exhibited" on May 26th 1884. In addition to the beacons, "*there were built, for the convenient service of the lights, 5,000 lineal feet of plank walk, two boat-houses and ten boat landings, two of them on palmetto piles.*" The Venus Point range lights were outfitted with white reflector locomotive lights, while the Elba Island lights featured fixed red locomotive headlights. All the other lights were outfitted with fixed red lanterns.[31] Work on completing the light stations was ongoing, however, as several were without keeper's dwellings.

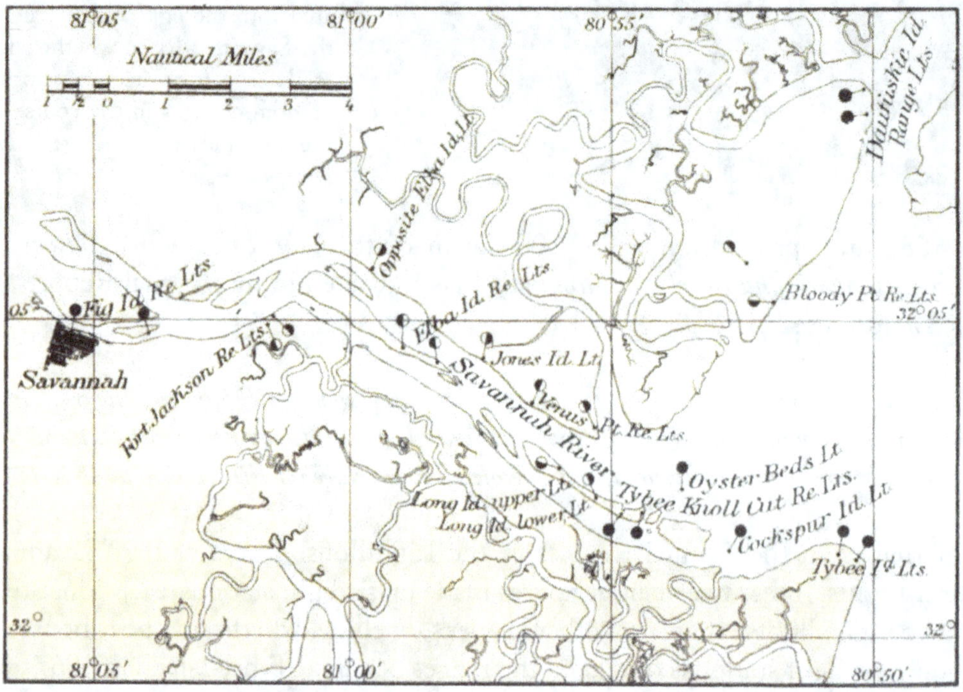

Savannah River Navigational System c1881
As depicted in an inset map of the Sixth District that appeared in the 1881 Annual Report of the Lighthouse Board (above) and as described in the 1884 report: "*On the completion of this system of lights, vessels can come in at night, by ranges, to a point inside Oyster Beds beacon, and leading lights will guide them from there to Fort Jackson, where two more ranges show them the way to the very wharfes of the city of Savannah.*"

Rear Beacon, Parris Island, S.C. c1881

This illustration of a range light – erected on Parris Island, South Carolina by officials of the Sixth District, was included in the Annual Report of the Lighthouse Board for 1881. This prefabricated iron beacon was the first of its kind and was the same type erected along the Savannah River during the early 1880s. These river lights were inexpensive, easy to build, and could be disassembled and re-used elsewhere if a light station was discontinued.

The following is a description of the Parris Island Range Lights from the book *The Modern Lighthouse Service* published in 1889: *"Altogether it is the most economical structure of its kind in the history of light-house construction. The plan was born of necessity, it being found that the appropriation made by Congress was not sufficient to put up the kind of structure which it was usual to place in such a position. … The light, which runs up and down in rails in the plane of the structure, is housed by day and at night is hoisted to its place at the apex of the triangle by machinery worked in the oil-house. The large foundation-plates are about 40 feet 4 inches apart. The focal plane of the light is 120 feet above the sea level, but the top of the structure is 132 feet from the ground. The cost of the iron work set up is $9,400, and that of the structure complete and lighted about $12,000."*[32]

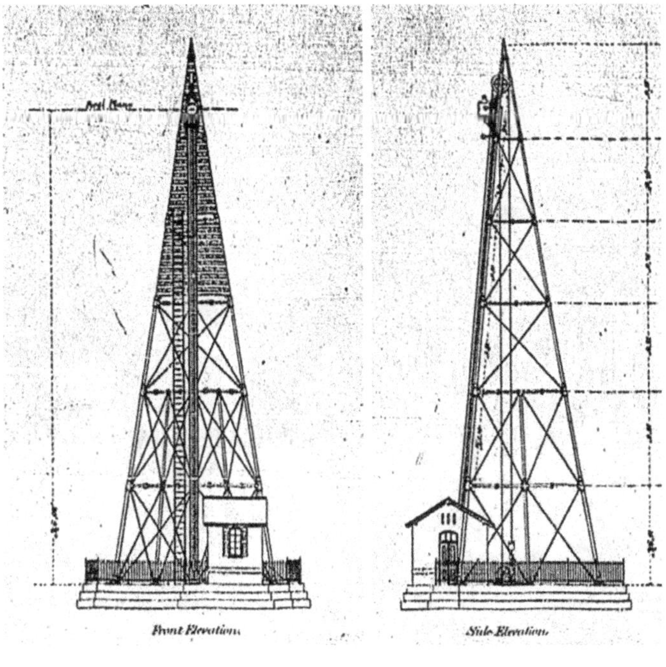

Venus Point Range Rear Light, Jones Island, Savannah River, South Carolina c1881.

These drawings of the iron beacon at Venus Point (at left) was completed in 1881 and is identical to the beacon at Parris Island and the beacons erected along the Savannah River. As indicated in the Annual Report of the Lighthouse Board for 1881, "*the locations for the lights were* (already) *selected and plans approved* – indicating that Sixth District officials had adopted and planned to implement this new type of lighthouse system wide as a standard for river navigation.

The contemporary photo at left is of the restored oil house of the Parris Island Range Rear Light – which was standard for this beacon type.[33]

Illustrations on the previous page and photograph courtesy of Kraig Anderson/Lighthouse Friends.

Jeremiah Keene (1884-1900) replaced George Martus as head keeper of the Cockspur Island/Oyster Beds Beacon Light Station in 1884 with Joseph L. Knight (1884-1885) serving as assistant keeper. Knight would be the first in a long succession of assistant keepers to serve during Keene's long tenure.[34]

In 1885 district officials were close to completing the light stations for the Savannah River Lights, reporting the construction of "*five substantial boat landings, with plank walks connecting them with their respective beacons*. In addition to this work, district officials also directed their attention to the maintenance and upkeep of the Cockspur Island Lighthouse. As reported in the *Annual Report of the Lighthouse Board* for 1885, "*the landing at the tower was strengthened, a boat landing was built on metal piles, 200 linear feet of plank walk were laid, and various minor repairs were made.*"

Cockspur Lighthouse c1885
In what appears to be a photo documenting the work completed in building the plank walk and boat landing reported in the *Annual Report of the Lighthouse Board*, this image may be the earliest photo of the Cockspur Lighthouse and perhaps the only one dating to the 19th century. The elevated plank walk and boat landing was vitally necessary for the keepers of the Cockspur Lighthouse as the light would need to be attended despite rough seas and high tides. *Photograph courtesy of the National Archives.*

In 1886 district officials directed their attention to much needed maintenance of the Oyster Beds Beacon, finally addressing recommended work that had been deferred for over a decade. From the *Annual Reports*:

> "*the shoal upon which this beacon stands was somewhat lowered by the current in Savannah River, which were caused by the construction of several stone wing-dams. A contract was therefore made for placing 185 cubic yards of stone as a talus around the base of the beacon to ... secure its foundation against the cutting effect of the current of the Savannah River.*"[35]

This work was carried out and proved successful as indicated in the 1888 *Annual Report*: *The stone was deposited and has checked the erosion of the shoal upon which the beacon stands.* The construction of the keeper's dwelling for the Elba Island Range Light Station in 1887 marked the completion of the Lighthouse Board's Savannah River Lights project. The dwelling – which cost $3,500 to build, was an example of the Lighthouse Service's standardized plan for keeper's quarters that was implemented at light stations in the Southeast during the 1870s and 1880s.[36] James Feely (1884-1887) – who served as assistant lighthouse keeper for the Cockspur/Oyster Beds Beacon Lighthouses under George Martus from 1881 to 1884, was the first head keeper at Elba Island and may have been the first to occupy the new dwelling. In 1887 George Martus became the second head keeper at Elba Island, a post he would serve until his retirement in 1931.[37]

Keeper's Dwelling - Elba Island Range Light Station
The Elba Island Range Lights Keeper's Quarters in a c1919 postcard. George Martus and his sister – Florence, lived here during his 44-year tenure as head keeper. Florence – the famed "Waving Girl," can be seen on the porch waving her handkerchief to a passing ship. Note the iron range rear beacon on the left side of the postcard.

As indicated in the *Annual Reports* for the late 1880s and early 1890s, changes in the current of the Savannah River led to extensive shoaling at light station boat landings, making the extension of the plank walks necessary, often as much as several 100 feet:

> *"... repairs to the elevated plank walk, equivalent to the renewal of 1,000 lineal feet, were made. In consequence of changes to the current of the Savannah River; caused by the construction of new jetties, the water near the head of the boat landing has shoaled so much that at low water the keeper's boat grounds at 75 feet from its head. It should be extended 100 feet into the river." – Tybee Knoll Cut Range*[39]

Tybee Knoll Cut Range Rear Light Boat Landing, photo c1915 - Devastating hurricanes in 1893, 1896, and 1898 wreaked havoc on the Savannah River light stations. The Tybee Knoll Cut Range Light Station was hit especially hard during the 1893 storm, with extensive damage to its plank walks and boat landings.[38] Note the three iron range beacons strategically aligned along the river channel. *Photograph courtesy of the National Archives.*

On the night of August 27, 1893, a powerful hurricane made landfall on Tybee Island, packing winds of 120 mph and a storm surge of 16 feet. The "Sea Islands" Hurricane of 1893 ranks as the 7th most deadly hurricane in United States history.[40] The keepers of the Cockspur and Oyster Beds Beacon Lighthouses – Jeremiah Keene and his assistant Charles Sisson, took refuge in the northwest stair tower of Fort Pulaski, where the men huddled for 10 hours as the storm pounded

Tybee and Cockspur Islands.[41] Light stations throughout the Sixth District were damaged by the massive and powerful storm, as indicated in the preamble of the district's report published in the *Annual Report of the Lighthouse Board* for 1893:

> *"It is necessary to state, before reporting in detail upon the work of the year, that this district, since the date of the last report, was visited by two storms of great severity. The first storm, in August 1893, was preceded by cyclones off the coast on the 15th, 20th, and 23d, and the high seas engendered by them culminated on August 27-28 in a tide in the Sixth light-house district higher by two feet than any which has been recorded. The center of the storm crossed the coast line between Savannah and Charleston leaving desolation in its course and causing, it is estimated, a loss of more than 2,000 lives on the sea islands of South Carolina. … On the Savannah River 5 barks were wrecked within a quarter mile of Tybee Knoll Cut front light … The Tybee beacon was undermined and overturned. The structures on the Tybee Knoll Cut front beacon, Elba Island front beacon, Bloody Point front beacon, Daufuskie Island front beacon and wharf at the rear, Hilton Head front beacon … suffered seriously, small structures being carried some distance from their foundations and larger ones being injured by wind and tide. Boat landings and elevated wooden plank walks, of which there are some miles in this district, suffered especially, and almost all of them required such extensive repairs as to make it economical to rebuild them. This was the case with the long wharves at Tybee Knoll Cut and Daufuskie Island light-stations …*

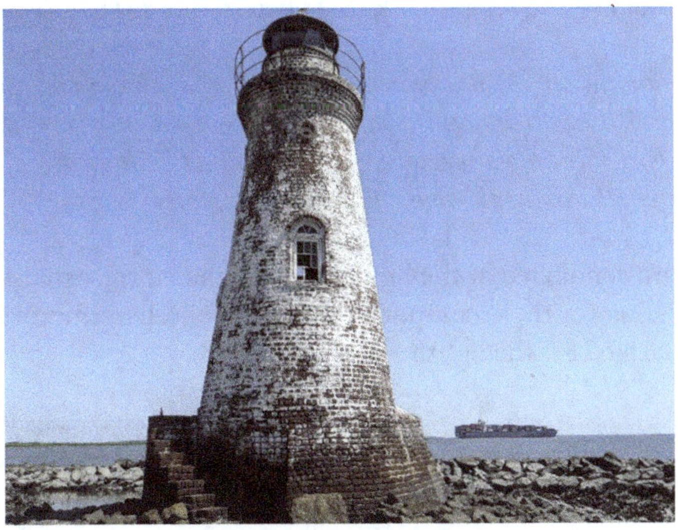

Photograph courtesy Friends of the Cockspur Lighthouse

As noted in the *Annual Report*, the lighthouse tender *Pharos* was engaged in repair and construction duty throughout the summer and fall of that year, making urgent repairs along the Savannah River at the Tybee, Tybee Knoll Cut, Venus Point, and Oyster Beds light stations.[42]

USLHT Pharos

Originally built as the schooner *H.H. Talman*, she was purchased by the Lighthouse Establishment in 1854 to serve as a lighthouse tender and renamed *Pharos*.[43] *Pharos* was first put into service as a supply tender in the Second Lighthouse District, delivering supplies along the east coast. After 1873 she served the Eighth and Fifth Lighthouse Districts. In 1890 she was transferred to the Sixth Lighthouse District. *Pharos* was the last sailing lighthouse tender in service when she was retired in 1907. She was named after one of the seven wonders of the ancient world: the Pharos Lighthouse in Alexandria, Egypt.[44] *Photograph courtesy of the U.S. Coast Guard Historian's Office.*

The Oyster Beds Beacon sustained considerable damage and required extensive repair, as indicated by the repair work described in the *Annual Report* for 1893.

> *"The boat landing at the beacon was repaired, and a new one, with boathouse, was built near the Fort Pulaski wharf. The doors and windows of the beacon were replaced, a part of the masonry tower was cut out and built up again, and the structure was strengthened by tie-rods ending in wall plates."*

Additional work conducted at the light station included the extension and repair of the boat landing for the Cockspur Lighthouse as well as improvements to the "temporary quarters" for the lighthouse keepers:

> *"Six casements in Fort Pulaski were fitted up with partitions, doors, windows and blinds, embrasure shutters, and closets for accommodation of the two keepers."*

The considerable repairs to the Oyster Beds Beacon and the construction of its own boat landing and boat house was part of the district's plans to establish a new range of lights. In 1895 the "Oyster Beds Range" lights were established with the

Oyster Beds Beacon serving as the rear range light and a newly constructed beacon located to the east serving as the front range light. This work was described in the *Annual Report* for 1895:

> *"a square structure of four piles, colored white, surmounted by a wooden pedestal arranged to show a fixed red lens lantern light of 90 degrees, 15 feet above mean high water, was built 2,000 feet to the seaward of Oyster Beds beacon to guide through the second or inner cut of the new dredged channel into the mouth of the Savannah River. It has not yet been lighted, a temporary light from a Funck lantern now being shown."*

The *Annual Report* for 1897 reported extensive damage to several Savannah River light stations caused by the "cyclone" of September 26, 1896. The boat landings and raised plank walks at Tybee Knoll Cut Range, Venus Point, and Jones Island "were seriously injured" by the hurricane and were completely rebuilt. No extensive damage was reported to the "Cockspur and Oyster Beds Range Light Station."

On October 2, 1898, Cockspur Island was visited by yet another devastating hurricane. As indicated in the *Annual Report* of 1899, damage to the Cockspur and Oyster Beds Range light station appears to have been moderate – mostly being limited to their respective boat landings, while the Tybee Knoll Cut and Elba Island Range light stations appear to have borne the brunt of the storm:

> *Tybee Knoll Cut – This station suffered severely from the storms of September and October, 1898. The superstructure of the wharf was renewed, a boathouse and about 1060 running feet of elevated plank walk was built. Various repairs were made.*
>
> *Elba Island – The site was literally buried in sedge brought by the storm tide of October, 1898, which covered the whole island. This was removed. The boat landing was repaired with 125 feet of plank walk. New lantern decks were put up for the beacons...*

In 1900 Jeremiah Keene was replaced by Edward L. Floyd (1900-1901) as head keeper at the Cockspur and Oyster Beds Range light station. Floyd's assistant keeper – Gustaf Ohman (1900-1901), succeeded him as head keeper a year later. Ohman (1901-1909) would become the last head keeper to serve the Cockspur Island Lighthouse.[45]

During the 1900s it appeared that the Lighthouse Board would finally erect a proper keeper's dwelling for the Cockspur and Oyster Beds Range light station after some prompting by the Sixth District officials. The *Annual Report of the Lighthouse Board* for 1900 included the observation that *"the quarters for the keeper of the Oyster Beds beacon and the keeper of Cockspur beacon are in the casements of Fort Pulaski fitted for the purpose. They are damp and unsatisfactory."* In 1902 the Treasury Department – on behalf of the Lighthouse Board, petitioned Congress for an appropriation to construct a new keeper's dwelling. The contents of the letter – dated January 11, 1902, from the Secretary of the Treasury to the Speaker of the House, was reprinted in the *Annual Report* for 1902:

> *"This Department has the honor to state, at the instance of the Light-House Board, that since the destruction by cyclone in 1881 of the dwelling then occupied by the keepers of the Cockspur and Oyster Beds range, Georgia, light-station, they have been quartered in the casements at Fort Pulaski, Georgia, which were temporarily fitted for this purpose.*
>
> *"These casements are damp, unsanitary, and unsuited to residential purposes, and it is impracticable to make them suitable for permanent habitation."*
>
> *The War Department has authorized the erection of a keeper's dwelling on the parapet at Fort Pulaski, Ga. This, it is estimated, can be done at a cost not exceeding $4,000.*
>
> *This Department concurs with the Board as to the urgent need for building a suitable dwelling for the use of the keepers of the Cockspur and Oyster beds range, Georgia, light-station, and recommends that an appropriation of $4,000 be made therefor."*

The letter was re-printed in the next several *Annual Reports*, to no avail. Rather than allocate the funds for a new dwelling, the War Department eventually authorized the use of the former ordinance sergeant's quarters in 1906, which was located on top of the parapet of Fort Pulaski.

The *Annual Report* for 1907 indicates that the "keeper's small dwelling" at Oyster Beds range was *"enlarged for use as a dwelling for both keepers. An hydraulic ram was installed for lifting water from the artesian well to the tank near the dwelling."*

As indicated in the *Annual Report* of 1905, several range lights along the Savannah River were to be discontinued and new ranges established as a result of a dredging project to create new shipping channels. The Long Island Crossing Range was completed and lit in August of 1905, and the Upper Flats and New

Fort Pulaski c1930s
Aerial photo of Fort Pulaski before its restoration by the CCC – the makeshift Cockspur and Oyster Beds range keeper's dwelling is barely discernable atop the fort. The dwelling is pictured below from another angle. Note the South Channel of the Savannah River at the top of the photo. *Photographs courtesty of the National Archives.*

Lower Flats ranges were under construction. The *Annual Reports* indicate that the Venus Point, Jones Island, and Elba Island ranges were to be discontinued once all the new ranges were completed. The light station buildings at Elba were to be occupied by the keeper of the Upper Flats range, and the buildings at Venus Point would accommodate the keepers of the Jones Island and Lower Flats ranges. The Oyster Beds range would also be affected:

> *"Oyster Beds range – The sixth order lens light in the rear beacon of this range will be discontinued when the new ranges now being built for Savannah Harbor are completed."*

As we know from later *Annual Reports*, the rear beacon – the Oyster Beds Beacon Lighthouse, was not discontinued at this time, nor was the Elba Island range light-station.[46]

By this time the deep draft ships navigating the Savannah River had begun using the North Channel exclusively.[47] In 1909 district officials recommended that the Cockspur Island Lighthouse be discontinued on June 1 of that year and that the beacon be maintained as a daymark.[48] In the *Annual Report* for 1909, "Cockspur Island – Sixth Order", was among several other obsolete lighthouses listed under the heading "Lights Discontinued."

The Oyster Beds range lights, however, remained operational. Records in the National Archives indicate that the Lighthouse Board changed the official name of the light station to the Oyster Beds Range Light-Station, Georgia, and Jones Island Range Lights, South Carolina – effective August 17, 1909.[49] It appears that the light station at Cockspur Island – and the Oyster Beds Beacon, did not remain in service much longer than the Cockspur Island Lighthouse. Lighthouse Service records indicate that Head Keeper Gustaf Ohman (1901-1912) was the last to serve in that post. He is believed to have served as head keeper until at least 1912.[50]

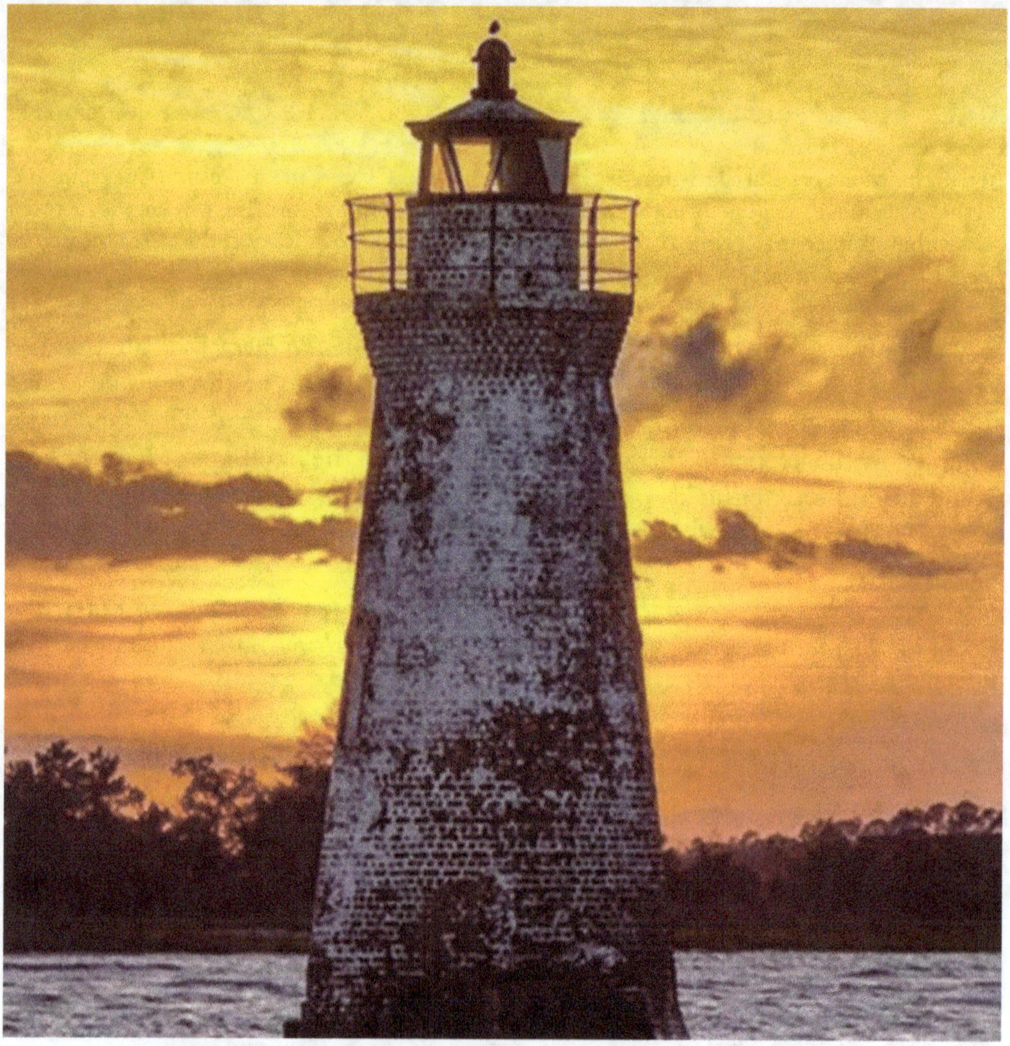

Photograph courtesy of the Friends of the Cockspur Island Lighthouse

The Keepers

Between 1848 and 1912, thirteen head lighthouse keepers are known to have been assigned to the Cockspur Island and Oyster Beds Beacons light station as well as over two dozen first assistant lighthouse keepers. These men – and one woman, along with their families, shared a common experience in their duties and living environments and belonged to a relatively small and unique community. Although the Sixth Lighthouse District encompassed the entire length of the South Atlantic coast of the United States – from New River Inlet, North Carolina, to and including Cape Canaveral, Florida, it appears that several of the Savannah River keepers were promoted or transferred within the area, serving at multiple light-stations over what was often a several-decades-long career. This was particularly true during the 1880s, when there were as many as eight light stations along the Savannah River.[1] Gustaf Ohman, for example, served as a first assistant lighthouse keeper at the Venus Point Range light-station from 1899-1900 before being transferred upriver to the Cockspur Island and Oyster Beds Range light-station in 1900. He was promoted to head keeper in 1901, serving in that capacity until 1912 when the light-station was discontinued. In 1913 Ohman was transferred downriver to the Tybee Knoll Cut Range

light-station where he briefly served as head keeper of the rear range light. Other examples are Hans Thorkildsen and Edward L. Floyd, both of whom served as first assistant lighthouse keepers at Cockspur Island before being promoted to head keepers at Tybee Knoll Cut Range light-station in 1895 and 1901, respectively. Floyd's tenure with the Lighthouse Board began with appointments at the Little Cumberland Island Lighthouse in McIntosh County, Georgia, followed by the Ponce De Leon Inlet Lighthouse in Ponce Inlet, Florida – an example of a keeper who did begin his career transferring throughout the Sixth District before settling in the Savannah River area. Floyd served as head keeper of the Tybee Knoll Cut light-station for 20 years, retiring in 1921.[2]

Cockspur Island Lighthouse c2021
View east of the Cockspur Island Lighthouse taken during the summer of 2021 when Fort Pulaski staff were in the process of stabilizing the beacon's masonry and repairing its door and windows - the Tybee Island Lighthouse is visible in the distance (at right). *Photograph courtesy of Ralph Eshelman, U.S. Lighthouse Society*

The Light Keepers Oath of Office

During the 1800s, each lighthouse keeper was required to take an oath before entering into service. The oath of office was administered by the Chief Clerk of the Lighthouse Inspector for each district. The following is the oath adopted by the Lighthouse Board:[3]

US LIGHT-HOUSE ESTABLISHMENT.
OATH OR AFFIRMATION OF LIGHT KEEPERS.

I, having been appointed ______ keeper of the ______ light at ______ in ______ do solemnly, sincerely, and truly swear (or affirm) that I will diligently and faithfully execute all the duties of the said office of ______ keeper of the said light _________ to the best of my ability and in strict conformity to the rules, regulations, instructions, and directions which have been or may be prescribed, and in obedience to all laws that have been or may be passed by Congress for the government and management of the United States Lighthouse Establishment service; and I further solemnly, sincerely, and truly swear (or affirm) that I will support the constitution of the United States.

Signature___________

Sworn or affirmed and subscribed this _____ day of _____ Anno Domini 18______
Before me

Signature___________

A Keeper's Life

According to lighthouse historian Candace Clifford, lighthouse keepers serving during the late 1920s were required by the Lighthouse Service (the successor agency to the U.S. Lighthouse Board after 1908) to fill out a form as part of the process to reclassify their pay structure. The forms required the lighthouse keepers to provide a description of their work duties at the light station as well as provide the number of years that they had served at that station. Housed in the National Archives, these forms provide a unique insight into what it was like to serve as a lighthouse keeper and the duties involved.[4] The following is the job description provided by lighthouse keeper Elmer Reed for the Negro Island Light Station in Camden, Maine – each description included an estimated percentage of working time:

40% My work at this station is to keep tower and all it contains in excellent condition at all times. This requires brushing, sweeping, polishing glass and brass, painting, fitting and trimming lamp, putting light out at sunrise and lighting at sunset, also changing light once during the night and putting in its place a full lamp.

40% Buildings to keep painted or whitewashed are dwelling house, shed, barn, boat house, and oil house and these are to be kept clean at all times. The grounds require regular cleaning and putting in order.

10% The bell for answering signals has to be rung everyday or night in answer to boat whistles during foggy weather.

5% I row a distance of about 1 mile for mail and provisions on suitable days.

5% Once each year I wheel the domestic coal from boat house to dwelling house in wheelbarrow, a distance of about 1000 feet. I make such repairs on station as I can. I assist disabled boats or aid anyone in distress. Monthly reports are made out and sent to district office as well as the annual property returns and requisitions.

Fort Jackson Range light-station c1915. An early 20th century view of the range beacon adjacent to the boat landing for this light station. Like all lighthouse keepers in the U.S. Lighthouse Service, the keepers of the Savannah River lights were responsible for maintaining the raised plank walks and boat landings as best they could. As indicated in the *Annual Reports*, the walks and wharfs associated with these light stations were frequently damaged by high tides and storms, and it could be many months before the lighthouse tenders could be deployed to the area to make repairs or rebuild these vital facilities. *Photograph courtesy the National Archives.*

While duties varied from light station to light station, the basic duties described by the Negro Point lighthouse keeper would have been fairly similar to those of keepers in other lighthouse districts. Climate and geography played a key factor in determining the type of experience a lighthouse keeper would have in performing his duties. For example, the Negro Point lighthouse is attached to the keeper's dwelling – which is fairly standard for northern lighthouses because of the harsh winters that are common there, while the lighthouses at the Cockspur Island and Oyster Beds Range light station are located in a sub-tropical climate on wave-swept islands that are located a great distance from its free standing keeper's dwelling. The Cockspur Island keepers would need to row twice daily to each lighthouse in order to maintain them, thus requiring the percentage of time required for this one task to be greatly increased compared to that of the Negro Point keeper.

Appointing Keepers

During the early 19th century lighthouse keepers were political appointees usually nominated by the collector of customs, who was also a political appointee. There was little regulation that defined a lighthouse keeper's qualifications and responsibilities. Little instruction and poor training were two good reasons for the varying quality of service given by early light keepers. Established in 1852, the U.S. Lighthouse Board laid the foundation for a career-oriented service for light keepers by instituting and enforcing a set of rules and regulations.[5] The appointment of keepers was restricted to:

> *"persons between the ages of 18 and 50, who can read, write, and keep accounts, are able to do the requisite manual labor, to pull a boat, and have enough mechanical ability to make necessary minor repairs about the premises, and keep them painted, whitewashed, and in order."*[6]

Nominees for light keeper were interviewed by district officials, and a three-month probationary period was also required before an appointment became permanent. In an effort to retain experienced personnel, keepers were allowed to transfer between stations and districts. Young men with sea experience were given priority as assistants for the larger light-stations, while retired sea captains or mates with families were often selected for stations requiring only one keeper.[7]

To remedy the lack of training and instruction not afforded the early keepers, the Lighthouse Board immediately set about providing written instructions: "Inspectors and light-keepers should be provided with printed instructions, in the form of manuals of instruction to guide them in the policing of the establishments."[8] The first of these manuals – *Instructions for Lightkeepers of the United States*, was published in 1852 and provided the information lighthouse keepers needed to properly operate a lighthouse while also setting a uniform standard for keepers to perform their duties throughout the Lighthouse Establishment. The first set of instructions was four pages long and was divided into two sections: one for light stations with one keeper and one for light stations with two keepers. By 1881 the manual had grown to 99 pages and included instructions down to the minutest of details.[9] Through thorough site inspections, good training, high standards, and enforcement of the regulations, the Lighthouse Board had succeeded in establishing a professional lightkeeper service by the late 1870s. Emblematic of this professionalism was the creation and issue of uniforms in 1884.[10] As stated in the 1885 *Annual Report*, the Lighthouse Board believed

> *"that uniforming of the personnel of the service, some 1,600 in number, will aid in maintaining its discipline, increase its efficiency, raise its tone, and add to its esprit de corps."*

Savannah River Light Keepers c1906
Wearing their Lighthouse Board-issued uniforms, keepers John H. Minges, James E. Swan, and Charles Armour are pictured sitting on the porch of the head keeper's cottage at the Tybee Island light station. Minges (1903-1917) and Swan (1901-1918) were both career light keepers serving at multiple light stations throughout the Sixth Lighthouse District. At the time of this photo, Minges was serving as 1st Assistant Lighthouse Keeper and Armour was assigned as 2nd Assistant at Tybee Island. In 1906 Swan was promoted to Principal Lighthouse Keeper of the Fort Ripley Shoal Lighthouse, Charleston, S.C.[11] *Photograph courtesy Tybee Island Historical Society.*

Photograph courtesy U.S. Lighthouse Society

The new dress uniforms – which were to be worn by all male lighthouse keepers, and officers of lightships and lighthouse tenders, consisted of a double-breasted coat, vest, trousers, and a cap in a dark indigo blue color. A yellow lighthouse badge was positioned in the center of the cap above the visor. A regulation apron was to be worn when cleaning lamps and lenses and an overall suit ("prescribed to save the uniform") was to be worn when repairing machinery and vessels. The uniform was to be worn at all times when on duty and when visiting the offices of the district officials. Lighthouse Service personnel were permitted to wear civilian clothing while away from the light station or when on private business – wearing civilian clothing with any part of the service uniform was strictly forbidden.[12]

Standardization within the Lighthouse Establishment was extended by the Lighthouse Board to all aspects of the service, beginning with personnel and lighthouse design – as discussed in Chapter 3, and later to the design of the keepers' dwellings. During the late 1870s, Lighthouse Board architects developed a design for a new keeper's dwelling that would become a standard for light stations along the South Atlantic coast between 1877 and 1907. First introduced at Cape Canaveral Light Station, Florida, in 1877, identical Stick-style keepers' dwellings were soon built at other Sixth District light stations such as Hilton Head Range, South Carolina, in 1880 and Tybee Island Range in 1881. Identical dwellings were built for the first assistant keepers at Cape Canaveral and Tybee Island light stations in 1883 and 1885, respectively. Iterations of this standard keeper's dwelling type

Cape Canaveral Assistant Keeper's Dwelling Pictured at left in 1894. Tybee Island Head Keepers Cottage pictured above c2020. *Photos courtesy of the National Archives and the author.*

were built at multiple Savannah River-area light stations during the 1880s, including Bloody Point Range on Daufuskie Island, S.C., Elba Island Range, and Tybee Knoll Cut Range.[13]

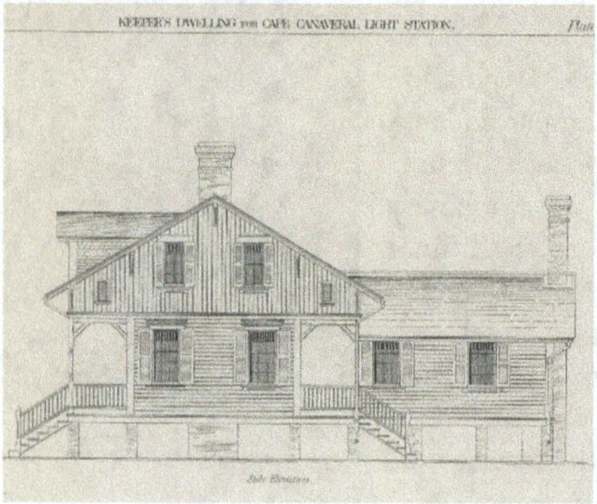

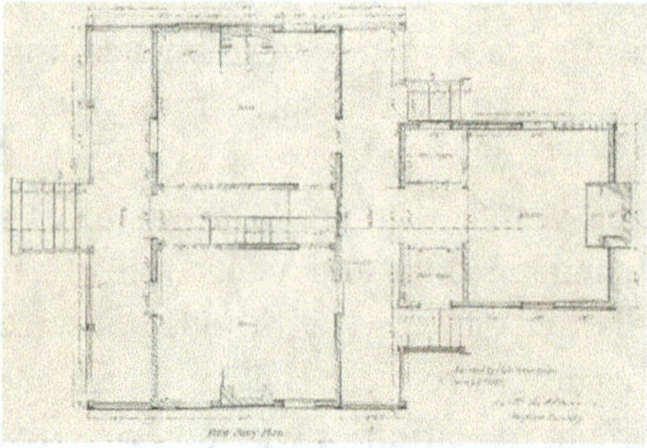

Cape Canaveral Head Keepers Dwelling, Side Elevation and First-Floor Plan c1877
Designed for the sub-tropical weather of the region, the style and design of these frame, one-and-a half story, center-hall type keeper's quarters became a standard for newly constructed housing for light stations along the South Atlantic coast during this period. Eighteen keeper's dwellings of this design are known to have been built at ten light stations in Florida, Georgia, South Carolina, and North Carolina. *"Adopted for Cumberland Island and Paris Island, April 1880"* is a notation made on one of the sheets for the Cape Canaveral plans, a written confirmation of its use as a standardized plan. Note the detached summer kitchen with open breezeway at the rear of the plan – a typical characteristic for 19th century houses of the region. *Images courtesy of the National Archives.*

Paul Johannes Pelz (1841-1918)
The first examples of the Stick style used by the U.S. Lighthouse Board were highly ornate integral lighthouses attributed to architect Paul J. Pelz. Pelz began as a draftsman for the Office of the U.S. Lighthouse Board in 1868 and served as Chief Draftsman from 1872 to 1877. His Stick-style designs for lighthouses included Hereford Inlet (1874), New Jersey, and Mare Island (1873), Point Fermin (1874), and East Brother (1874) in California. Pelz is also credited with designing numerous U.S. Life-Saving Service stations during the 1880s.[14] His Stick-style designs were often utilized in popular resort areas similar to places like Tybee Island. As Chief Draftsman, Pelz likely had a hand in designing the Keeper's Dwelling for the Cape Canaveral Light Station. Although the design is a more scaled-down, utilitarian version of the Stick style than what he is known for, what became a standard design for the Lighthouse Board bears many elements of his known works.
Photograph courtesy of the Library of Congress

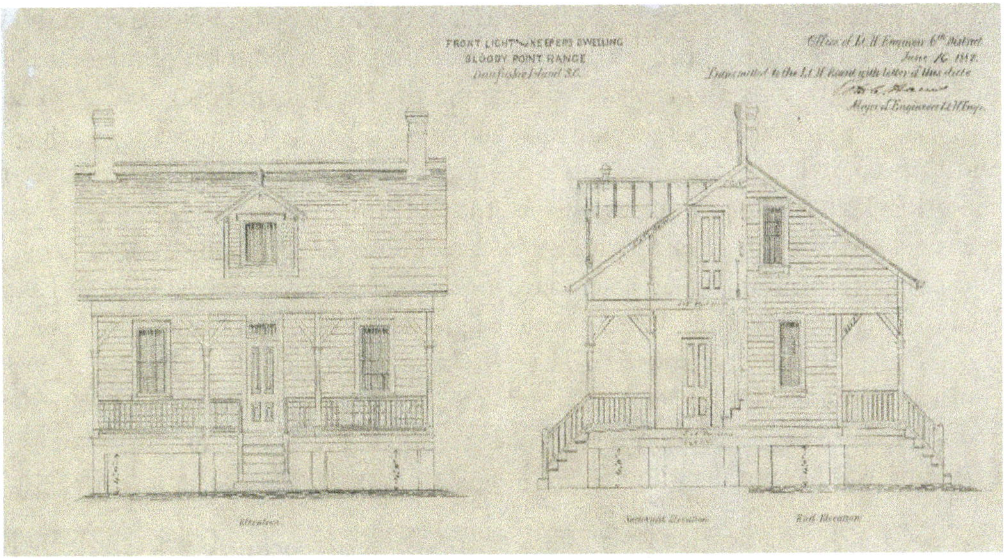

Front Light and Keeper's Dwelling, Bloody Point Range, Daufuskie Island, S.C. c1882.
An austere iteration of the standard type built on a remote island – the gable has been adapted to house the light.

Elba Island Range Keepers Dwelling (left) and Cape Fear Keepers Dwelling, North Carolina
Postcard c1910 courtesy Live Oak Public Library; c1903 drawing courtesy of the National Archives

Cape Fear Keeper's Dwelling c1903
Side elevation at left. *Image courtesy of the National Archives.*

By the mid to late 1880s the Lighthouse Board began to commission a simplified version of the standard keeper's dwelling, retaining the basic form of the original design but eschewing all ornament other than the Stick-style porch brackets and posts, as exemplified by the dwellings at Elba Island Range Light Station (c1887) and Cape Fear Light Station, North Carolina (c1903).[15] It is likely that each of the other light stations built as part of the "Savannah River Lights" project of the early 1880s – Jones Island Range, Venus Point Range, Long Island Range, and Fort Jackson Range, had a standard-design keeper's dwelling similar to Elba Island Range light station. With so many light stations to accommodate, it is not surprising that the Cockspur Island and Oyster Beds Beacon light station was consistently denied allocations for a new keeper's dwelling throughout the 1880s and 1890s – the availability of Fort Pulaski's casements as an alternative accommodation was likely a deciding factor.

Cape Fear Light Station, North Carolina
The first-order Cape Fear light station was comprised of a 150-feet tall skeletal tower, three keeper's dwellings, two storage buildings, and a brick generator building located at the foot of the tower. The ordered and uniform layout of the station reflects the military background of the officers that dominated the Lighthouse Board and the officials under whose authority each district was administered. This photo was taken in 1952. *Photograph courtesy of the U.S. Coast Guard.*

Most light stations on land feature a beacon, keeper's dwelling, and an oil storage building, as well as a wharf or boat landing, boat house, possibly a fog-signal building, and other miscellaneous outbuildings.[16] Depending on its size and complexity, a light station could have as many as five keepers.[17] Smaller stations – such as the "sixth-order" Cockspur Island and Oyster Beds Range light station, only required one "head keeper" and one first assistant keeper – one keeper per beacon. A "first-order" light station – which features a lighthouse equipped with the largest lens, required at least three keepers to operate effectively. Because the large Fresnel lens of a first-order lighthouse required constant attention during the night and frequent cleaning during the day, multiple keepers were required to cover the necessary work in shifts.[18]

Tybee Island Light Station as viewed from the lighthouse, Head Keeper's & First-Assistant Keeper's Dwellings
The formal quadrangle arrangement of the lighthouse and the three keeper's dwellings (at left) is a reflection or segment of the Confederate/Union garrison that existed at this site during the Civil War. In 1867 the second-assistant keeper's dwelling was built on the site of the former barracks building. In 1881 the existing head keeper's dwelling was built in line with the lighthouse at the east end of the quadrangle. The engineers that served the Lighthouse Board were often officers, so it was not unusual that a continuation of the formal military quadrangle would be ordered.[19]

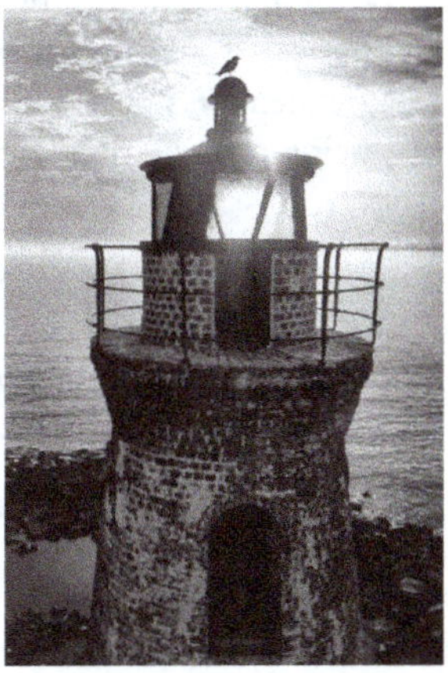

Keeping the Watch – Cockspur Island Lighthouse
It was the responsibility of the keeper on watch to make sure the light shined bright and clear throughout the night while also remaining vigilant for distressed mariners. In larger lighthouses the keeper would perform his duty from the "watch room" – the room beneath the lens room which also featured its own gallery for keeping a lookout for ships. Since the Cockspur Island Lighthouse does not feature a watch room, these functions were likely carried out from the lantern room and gallery. *Photograph courtesy Frank Logue.*

Regardless of the number of keepers assigned to a light station, the lamps were to be lighted punctually every day at sunset and extinguished at dawn. During this time, light keepers were to keep a "regular and constant watch throughout the night." First watch was kept between 8:00 p.m. and midnight, and the second watch from midnight to 4:00 a.m. As a basic rule, the duration of a watch would not exceed 4 hours.[20] In caring for the maintenance and upkeep of the lighthouses, the Lighthouse Board's *Instructions and Directions to Light Keepers* divided the daily work schedule for lighthouses with two or more keepers and only one light-room into two shifts, or "departments":

> *First Department*: The keeper or keepers having charge of the first department shall, immediately after the completion of the duties of the keeper of the morning watch, clean and polish the lens or other apparatus, clean and fill the lamp; remove all dust with the feather brushes from the frame-work of the apparatus; fit new wicks, if required, and, if not required, trim carefully those already fitted in the burner; and see that everything connected with the apparatus and lamp is perfectly clean, and the light ready for lighting at the proper time in the evening.

> *Second Department*: The keeper or keepers having charge of the second department shall, immediately after the completion of the duties by the keeper of the morning watch, clean the plate-glass of the lantern inside and outside; clean all the copper and brass work of the apparatus; the utensils used in the lantern and watch room; the walls, floors, and balconies of the lantern; the revolving machinery, if any; the tower stairways, landings, doors, windows, window recesses, and passages from the lantern to the oil cellars.[21]

Instruction #43 applied directly to light stations like the Cockspur and Oyster Beds Beacon Light Station, where there were two lights, but only two keepers at the station:

> "… both keepers will, at … half an hour before sunset, proceed each to one of the lanterns, prepare for lighting, light the lights, and remain each in his lantern until the light is fully exhibited and burning steadily at its greatest height. The keeper whose regular watch it may be at that time will then take charge of the lights and employ his time in visiting each light as frequently as necessary during the remainder of the watch. The unattended light for the time being must be frequently looked at from the occupied lantern."[22]

It would have been challenging – and impractical, for the keepers of the Cockspur and Oyster Beds Beacon Lighthouses to have carried out these instructions given that each would have to row to their assigned lighthouse – one at considerable distance, light the lights, and then one keeper would be expected to tend to both lights during his four-hour watch, at some point rowing to the second light to ensure that it was functioning properly (a task that was indeed carried out solely by the first four keepers at Cockspur Island). It is more likely that the keepers tended to one beacon each given the logistics of a shared responsibility that would seem to have created an unnecessary amount of additional work.

First-Order Fresnel Lens, Point Reyes Lighthouse, California – *Image courtesy of the U.S. Lighthouse Society*

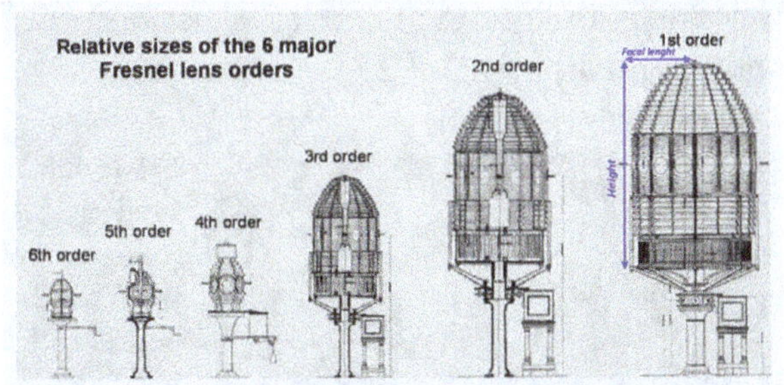

Diagram illustrating the range of sizes between the smallest Fresnel lens and the largest – *Courtesy www.enschrage.nl*

The 6th-Order Fresnel lenses that were installed in the Cockspur Island and Oyster Beds Beacon lighthouses were much easier to maintain than a 1st-Order Fresnel lens as the 6th-Order lens was much smaller and was therefore easier to clean and service. The surface glass of a 1st-Order lens alone would take two men to clean effectively while its lantern room – which also required cleaning, would need to be large enough to accommodate such a large and complex apparatus. By comparison, the lens room and apparatus of a 6th-Order lighthouse is considerably smaller, as the Fresel lens is only 17 inches in height.[23]

Family Life

The Lighthouse Board preferred to appoint married men to positions of keeper because they were considered more reliable than single men. As a result, many isolated light stations were inhabited not only by the keeper, but also his wife and children.[24] Such was the case of John H. Lightburn – a seaman who was the first lighthouse keeper appointed to the Cockspur Island and Oyster Beds Beacons light station in 1849. John – who was 35 years old, and his wife Caroline – who was 30 years old, had four children that lived with them at the keeper's dwelling at the southeast end of Cockspur Island near the South Channel: William (12 y/o); Mortimer (9 y/o); John (5 y/o); and Francis (10 mos.). At 10 months old, Francis was likely the first child born at the light station but would be far from the last.[25] Another lighthouse keeper family – the Keane's, resided in the temporary quarters within the casements of Fort Pulaski from 1884 to 1900. Jeremiah was 39 when he was first appointed head keeper – at the time he and his wife Maggie had three children ranging from five to one years old. That first year they welcomed a new son at the light station – William, followed by Robert in 1887 and Jeremiah, Jr, in 1892.[26]

Frederick H. Bruggeman
Frederick Bruggeman – a native of Germany, was a seasoned veteran of the Lighthouse Service by the time he was appointed principal keeper of the Tybee Island Range light station in 1914. He began his light-keeping career at Little Cumberland Island Lighthouse, McIntosh County in 1901, where he served as 1st assistant keeper. His wife Anna and 9-year-old son William came with him to the light station where a second son – Charles, was born in 1902. The growing family moved to South Carolina in 1905 when Frederick was promoted to principal keeper of the Hilton Head Range light station. Their daughter Martha was born at this light station in 1908. In 1913 the family moved to Hunting Island, South Carolina, where Frederick served as principal keeper for one year. Frederick's eldest son – William, began working under his father in 1919 when he was appointed 2nd assistant light keeper at the Tybee Island Range light station. Frederick resigned his commission as principal keeper at Tybee Island in 1931, retiring from the Lighthouse Service at the age of 69.[27] *Photograph courtesy of the Tybee Island Historical Society.*

Not all light keepers were married – the Lighthouse Board also gave preference to retired sea captains and young men with sea experience – particularly in serving in an assistant keeper position.[28] The second head keeper at the Cockspur and Oyster Beds Beacon light station was James Callan – an unmarried retired sea captain who only served in the position for one year.[29]

According to Dennis L. Noble in his book *Lighthouses and Keepers*, keepers and their families "faced both boredom and danger." Some of the danger stemmed from accidents on the job or sickness at an isolated location where immediate medical care was not available. Most of the danger, however, came from the elements: hurricanes and storms, high tides, and occasionally, distressed mariners needing aid – none of which relieved the keeper of his duties. As was often the case, the keeper's wife – and sometimes older children, aided him in some of his duties around the station. At stations where there was only one keeper, it was quite common for the keeper's wife to assume a watch following her husband's shift to allow him some rest before attending to his other duties later in the day.[30]

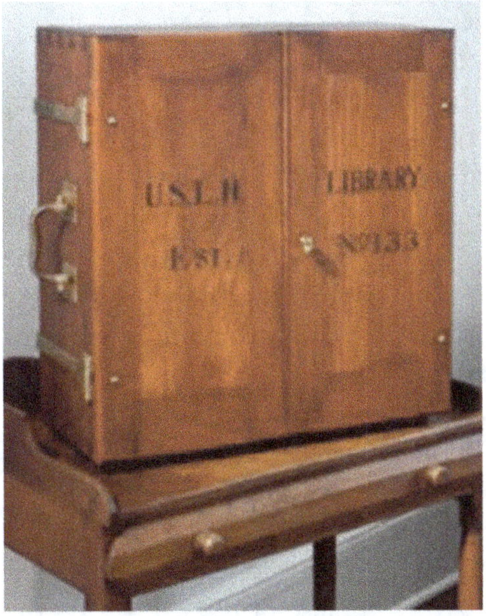

To help keepers and their families combat the boredom often associated with remote, isolated light stations, the service encouraged the cultivation of gardens. In 1876, the Lighthouse Board introduced portable libraries that contained about 40 books and magazines covering a wide variety of subjects, from history to science as well as poetry. Each library was numbered and contained in a sturdy wooden box that was changed out following each quarterly inspection.[31] By 1884, 380 libraries were being circulated amongst the stations.[32]

Reproduction U.S. Lighthouse Establishment Portable Library – St. Simons Island Keepers Dwelling *Photograph courtesy of the Coastal Georgia Historical Society*

Many children of light keepers – having spent their childhoods growing up at a light station, often followed in their father's footsteps, either becoming keepers themselves or living lives in service to the sea. Such is the case of the Egan Family – who lived in and served Savannah River light stations during the 1850s through the 1880s. Patrick and his wife Anne immigrated to the United States from Ireland in 1854. Patrick was appointed head keeper of the Cockspur Island and Oyster Beds Beacon light station in 1856. At the time, he and his wife Anne had one child – one-year-old John. By the end of Patrick's first appointment to the Cockspur light station in 1867, the family had grown to include two more sons – Thomas and Michael, and a daughter – Maria. Patrick's second appointment as head keeper at Cockspur Island lasted from 1868 until 1877. In 1869 the family had welcomed a fourth son – James. Records indicate that the eldest Egan boys had begun working at the light station as "boatsmen" by the late 1860s. Three of the Egan sons served as assistant light keepers under their father: John Egan (1867-1870; 1875-1876) and Thomas Egan (1870-1871) as first assistant light keeper at the Cockspur Island and Oyster Beds Beacon light station; and Michael Egan (1878) as second assistant light keeper at the Tybee Island Range light station, where Patrick served as head keeper from 1877 to 1881.[33]

The Martus family is probably the most well-known of all the families associated with the Savannah-River-area lighthouses. In 1842, John Martus immigrated with his parents from Baden-Wurttemberg, Germany.[34] In 1866, Sgt. Martus – a decorated disabled veteran, was assigned the post of Ordinance Sergeant at Fort Pulaski during the period of its repair and modernization (1866-1873). Sgt. Martus brought his pregnant wife Rosanna and their four children to Cockspur Island where they lived in the former quarters of the engineer officers in the Fort Village. Two daughters were born on Cockspur Island – Mary Alfreta in 1866 and Florence in 1868.[35] The Martus children grew into adulthood on Cockspur Island where the coming and going of passing ships was an everyday occurrence. By the early 1870s, plans to continue the modernization of Fort Pulaski were scrapped. In 1873 the last remaining garrison at Fort Pulaski was withdrawn, leaving behind Sgt. Martus as part of a small caretaker detail.[36]

In 1877, John's eldest son – 16 years old George W. Martus, was appointed first assistant lighthouse keeper at the Cockspur Island Lighthouse.[37] John Martus continued in his capacity as Ordinance Sergeant at Fort Pulaski until 1880 when Fort Pulaski was officially decommissioned as a military reservation – an action that coincided with his discharge from the Army because of ill health.[38] As the eldest son, George continued to provide for his family as a light keeper, being promoted to head keeper of the Cockspur Island and Oyster Beds Beacon light station in 1881.[39] In 1884 George resigned his post as head keeper at Cockspur Island and moved the family into Savannah, most likely because of his father's failing health.[40]

"Waving Girl" – Elba Island Keeper's Dwelling, photo undated.
Courtesy lighthousefriends.com

After John's death, George was appointed head keeper of the Elba Island Range light station in 1887 – a position in which he would serve until 1931. The remainder of the Martus family – his mother Rosanna and his youngest sister Florence, lived with him at the small frame keeper's dwelling facing the Savannah River. It was here that Florence would become internationally famous as Savannah's "Waving Girl," as no ship calling on Savannah between 1887 and 1931 is said to have passed their little white dwelling on Elba Island without her waving a handkerchief by day or a lantern by night.

As her fame spread, seamen on vessels entering the harbor would watch for and anticipate seeing the "Waving Girl" and would return her greeting with a toot of their whistle or siren as they passed.[41] By the 1900s Florence's ritual was well known, as evidenced by an article published in the *Savannah Morning News* on January 31, 1904, entitled "The Lone Light House Girl: Story of Miss Martus and Her Life on Elba Island." Decades later – as her legend grew, there would be much romanticized speculation as to why Florence began and continued her daily vigil. This early article, however, dispels many of those myths and provides a clear explanation from the "Light House Girl" herself, in her own words:

> "*The ships are my friends,*" says Miss Martus. "*Of course I have a few friends in the city, and occasionally we come to visit them, but I am always homesick for my home among the marshes, and for my ships. I love them so. I do not believe that any other little girl was ever so proud of her dolls or loved them so dearly as I did my ships when I was a little bit of a thing. When girls grow up to be women they get over the dolls of their babyhood, but my love for my ships has never abided, and I shall always love them.*
>
> *The captains and the crews are good to me, too. I know it must be troublesome for them to speak to me as they do, far across the water, but I am also sure that they do not grudge me the favor, for they must know how I love the ships and how it cheers me in my loneliness to have them acknowledge my salutes. I think of the terrors of the deep when I see my brave ships passing. When one is going out to sea I pray for her safe passage; pray that she may reach her port. I have learned to know the ships. I can tell them all from a distance, even as a sailor might, and I feel like some loved friend or relative had returned to me from some perilous experience as I see the brave craft come slowly up the river.*"[42]

"Light House Girl" Postcard c1910
Florence was also referred to as "The River Queen," and later, "The Waving Girl." George and Florence's mother – Rosanna, kept house at their Elba Island dwelling until her death in 1909. At the time of her passing, the local maritime community held Florence in such high regard that passenger ships entering the harbor flew their flags at half-mast in honor of her mother, and a tugboat was dispatched to Elba Island to transport the family to the city on the day of the funeral.[44] *Postcard courtesy of Live Oak Public Library*

Florence's love for the ships and the seamen who sailed them was reciprocated by the maritime community. Every Christmas the Ocean Steamship Company, the Merchants and Miners Transportation Company, the Savannah Pilots Association, and the tugboat companies would send Florence "Christmas boxes" as tokens of their esteem for her. Florence also received gifts and letters from seamen from all over the world.[43]

While census records list Florence's role at the light station as "keeping house," it has been well documented that she often assisted her brother George with his duties at the light station in addition to taking part in multiple life-saving rescues over the decades. The most well-known rescue occurred in the early hours of October 27, 1911. At 4:30 in the morning, Florence had risen to greet a passing ship with a wave of her lantern when she heard the cries of the distressed seamen of dredge No. 15, which had caught fire, causing the thirty-two members of the crew to abandon the flaming hulk. Eight men piled into a pontoon moored to the side of the dredge and pushed away without oars and any means of guiding the boat. Hearing their cries as the boat was being carried out to sea, Florence rowed to the scene and towed the boat back to the light station. Together with her brother, George, the siblings collected the rest of the men from the marsh. Thirty-one were rescued and returned to Savannah the following day. News of the dramatic rescue and the heroic actions of the "Waving Girl" was picked up by newspapers across the country, amplifying Florence's fame even more.[44]

George and Florence Martus c1911
Courtesy of the Georgia Historical Society

After George retired in 1931, he and Florence moved to Bona Bella – a marshside community on the outskirts of Savannah. The 1931 *Annual Report of the Lighthouse Board* noted the occasion with the following citation: *"Miss Florence Martus, widely known to seafaring men and to those who travel in ships, as Savannah's "waving girl," has given her last salute to vessels entering and leaving the port of Savannah. Miss Martus, a central figure of romance woven about lonely Elba Island, on which she has lived for nearly a half century, plans to move to Savannah, as her brother, George W. Martus, keeper of the light, has just retired. He has tended the lights along the Savannah River since 1887."*

On her 70th birthday, the city of Savannah gave Florence a birthday party at Fort Pulaski which was attended by over 4,000 people.[45] George died in 1940 at the age of 79. Florence died three years later at the age of 74. A Liberty Ship – the SS Florence Martus, was named in her honor. As a final tribute to Florence, "The Waving Girl" statue was erected on River Street in Savannah in 1972.

Diversity in the Ranks: Women and African-American Lightkeepers

Well into the 20th century, all maritime professions in the United States were dominated by men. Most employees of the U.S. Lighthouse Service were white men. However, recent scholarship has revealed a previously unknown diversity among the ranks of the keepers. African-Americans played a role in the service that has largely gone unrecorded, although official records exist that show their appointment as both head and assistant keepers.[46] Likewise, a surprising number of women were employed as keepers by the service. In their book *Women Who Kept the Lights,* lighthouse historians Mary Louise Clifford and J. Candace Clifford list 240 women who served as assistant keepers as well as the appointments of 138 women as head keepers.[47] Author Dennis L. Noble maintains that the service's motivation to hire women "did not spring from some enlightened equal employment policy." Rather – as he posits in his book *Lighthouses and Keepers,* the service took advantage of the labor that was already provided by the family of male head keepers. Like Florence Martus and countless other family members living at light stations, children and women learned the business of running a lighthouse over time and often performed tasks to assist the keeper, essentially acting as unpaid first-assistant keepers. A death of a husband or father might lead to a woman becoming a head keeper temporarily until a replacement arrived – much like Mary Maher who succeeded her husband at Cockspur Island following his death from drowning in 1853, a post that appears to have become permanent as she remained head keeper until 1856.[48]

While Mary Maher's role as a head keeper is well-known, new research has revealed that more than a half dozen women served the Savannah River lights as keepers. Scouring U.S. Lighthouse Service records, Kelsey Chandler – archivist for the Tybee Island Historical Society, compiled an impressive list of female keepers of whom little was previously known. As Chandler points out in her writings, most of these women worked alongside their husbands, who often held a higher rank. One of these women was Eliza Morel. In 1878 she was appointed first assistant keeper at the Tybee Knoll Cut Range light station alongside her husband – head keeper Thaddeus Morel. The Morels were the first keepers assigned to the station – a commission that they retained until their joint resignation in 1881. Thaddeus and Eliza are the only African-American light keepers known to have been appointed to serve in the Savannah area.[49]

Tybee Knoll Cut Range Light Station c1878
The Morels lived on Cockspur Island at a time when the only other occupants were the light keepers, their families, and Dr. J.P. Huger, who served as Quarantine Officer. The other light keepers included Charles Poland – head keeper of the Cockspur Island and Oyster Beds Beacon Range light station, his wife Ellen, and the family of George Martus –who served as his first assistant keeper. Also living with the Morels was their 10-year-old daughter Josephine and Thaddeus's sister, Virginia. Josephine would have been around the same age as the youngest Martus girls – Mary, 14, and Florence, 12.[50] *Drawing courtesy of the National Archives.*

Maria C. Johnson is another female light keeper highlighted by Chandler's research. Johnson succeeded Eliza Morel as first assistant lightkeeper at the Tybee Knoll Cut Range light station. She and her husband John – who was appointed head keeper, were both natives of Sweden. Both Maria and her predecessor received a salary of $400 – a sum commensurate with their male counterparts. She served in this post from 1881 until her death in 1887. It is unknown whether her death was the result of illness or was job-related. Her husband John remained as head keeper until 1894 with their son, Gustaf, serving as his first assistant.[51]

Chandler's work reveals that at least five women served as keepers at the Tybee Island Range light station between 1869 and 1889. Emma Manchester (1870) and Alice H. Evans (1889) both had brief tenures as assistant lighthouse keepers. Alice Evans was appointed first assistant keeper following the death of her husband, the head lighthouse keeper – a common occurrence in the Lighthouse Service in which a keeper's wife served in her husband's place temporarily until a replacement could be assigned. Francis Sickel (1870-1873) was appointed first assistant light keeper under her husband George Sickel – who served as head keeper from 1870 to 1873. Mrs. M. L. Cohen also worked alongside her husband – Head Keeper William H. Cohen. Mrs. Cohen was appointed second assistant keeper in 1869, serving in that capacity until her death the following year. Another husband-and-wife team were career light keepers Bridget and Patrick Comer. The Comers transferred to Tybee Island in 1873, having most recently served as head keeper and first-assistant keeper at the light station at Combahee Bank, South Carolina (1868 – 1873). During their brief tenure at Tybee Island (1873), Patrick was appointed head keeper and Bridget second assistant keeper. Later that same year they were transferred to the Daufuskie Island Rear, S.C., light station (1873-1891) with Bridget appointed first-assistant keeper under Patrick, who was appointed principal keeper.[52]

Laura and George Jackson c1940
Principal Keeper George B. Jackson, his wife Laura, and their five children lived at the Tybee Island Range light station from 1931 to 1947. Whether they were officially employed by the Lighthouse Service or were the wives or daughters of the keepers, the contributions of women at light stations across the country were immeasurable. *Photograph courtesy of the Tybee Island Historical Society.*

Cockspur Island and Oyster Beds Beacon Light Station

Head Keeper

John H. Lightburn		–	1849
James Callan		–	1850
Cornelius Maher	1851	–	1853
Mary Maher	1853	–	1856
Thomas Quinliven		–	1856
Patrick Egan	1856	–	1867
Thomas F. Floyd	1867	–	1868
Patrick Egan	1868	–	1877
Charles W. Poland	1877	–	1881
George W. Martus	1881	–	1884
Jeremiah Keane	1884	–	1900
Edward L. Floyd	1900	–	1901
Gustav Ohman	1900	–	1912

First Assistant Keeper

James Cullen	1857	–	1859
Joseph Smith	1866	–	1867
John Egan	1867	–	1870
Thomas Egan	1870	–	1871
Robert Egan	1871	–	1875
John Egan	1875	–	1876
William Jackson	1876	–	1877
George W. Martus	1877	–	1881
James Feeley	1881	–	1884
Peter Johnson		–	1884
Joseph J. Knight	1884	–	1885
August Haine	1885	–	
Lucien H. Raines		–	1886
Gustav H.W. Denrell	1886	–	1888
Harrick Lehman	1888	–	1891
Hans Thorkildsen	1891	–	1892
John Linquist	1892	–	1893
Joseph S. Estell		–	1893
Charles S. Sisson	1893	–	1895
Burwell M. Floyd	1895	–	1897
Fred T. Sisson	1898	–	1900
Gustav Ohman	1900	–	1901
Anander Loverson	1901	–	1903
Carl Anderson	1903	–	1906
Edward B. Magwood	1906	–	1909
Gabriel N. Jackson	1909	–	1911

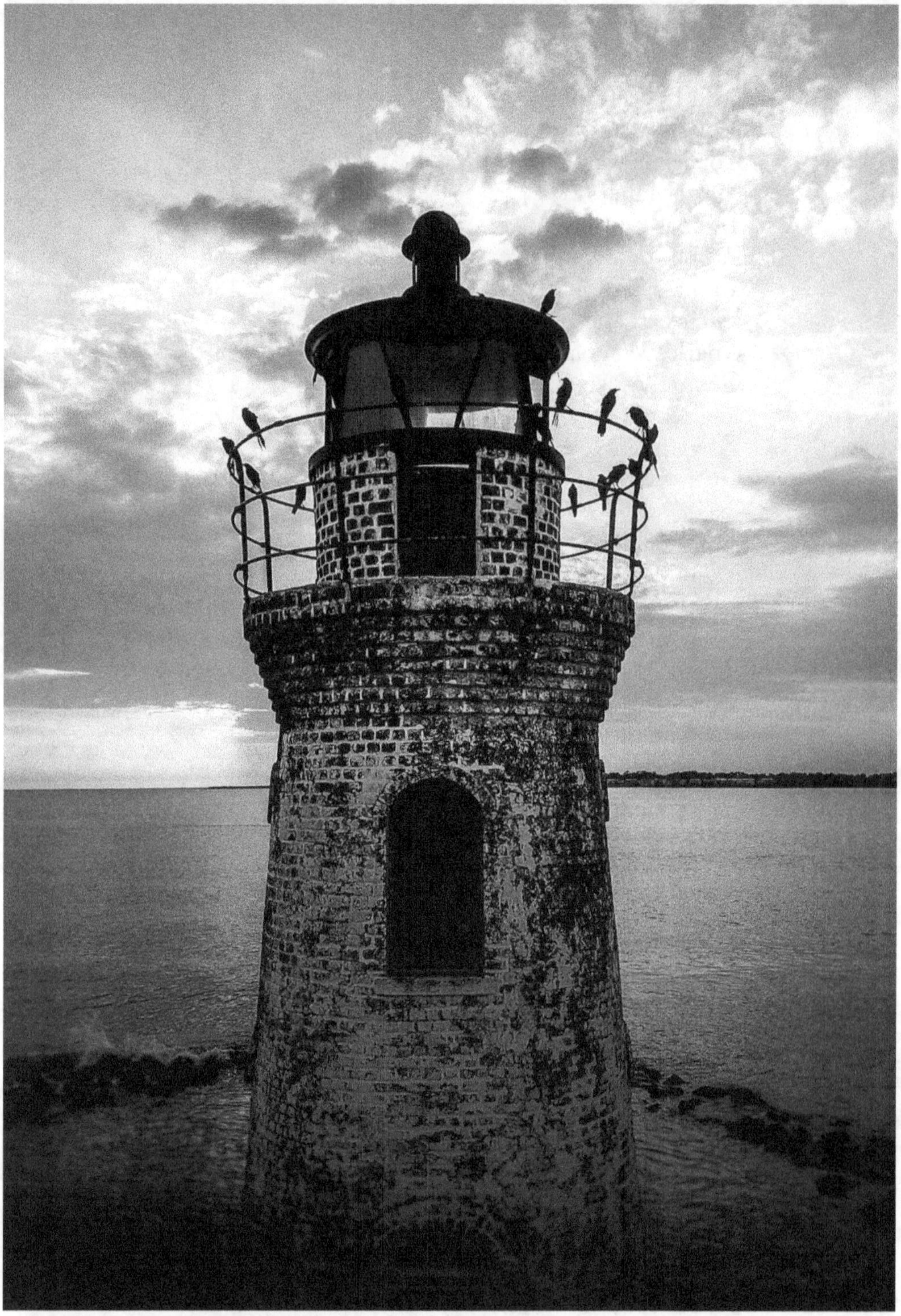

Cockspur Lighthouse c2016 - *Photograph courtesy of Frank Logue*

Chapter Six

The Daymark

Following its deactivation in 1909, the Cockspur Island Lighthouse was maintained as a daymark by the Lighthouse Service and its successor – the U.S. Coast Guard, until its abandonment in 1949.[1]

Interest in the lighthouse becoming a part of the Fort Pulaski National Monument originated with Ralston B. Lattimore – Historical Technician for the Office of National Parks, Buildings, and Reservations in Savannah, when he wrote to the Director of the National Park Service in 1937 recommending that the lighthouse be acquired *"because of its picturesque value and to protect the monument from the possibility of a fishing camp being established there."* Correspondence between the Director of the National Park Service and the Commissioner of Lighthouses later that same year indicated a willingness to transfer the titles to Cockspur Point and Oyster Bed Island on the condition that the beacons be maintained *"as valuable landmarks and guides to mariners entering the Savannah River."*[2]

The events of World War II postponed any further discussion of the island until 1949, when a private party expressed interest in purchasing the islet on which the Cockspur Lighthouse was situated for use as a "weekend spot." This inquiry set in motion a concerted effort by National Monument and National Park Service officials to secure and protect the lighthouse and islet in the belief that the *"sale of this item to private parties for exploitation or for salvage operations would be most embarrassing to the monument"* and would completely ruin the historic aspect of the park. Writing in 1955, Ralston B. Lattimore provided the following description of significance to justify the transfer of the islet and beacon to the Fort Pulaski National Monument:

> *"Cockspur Light ... constructed in the 1830s of brick and stone and enlarged in 1856, was an established landmark on Cockspur Point between the fort and the Federal batteries at the time of the battle in 1862. It is therefore contemporary with the fort and is an interesting architectural survival."*[3]

In 1958 the one-acre "Cockspur Island Lighthouse Reservation" and the small oyster shell reef known as "Daymark Island" were transferred by Presidential Proclamation from the U.S. Coast Guard to the Fort Pulaski National Monument.[4] In 1960, Cockspur's sister beacon and the one-acre Oyster Bed Lighthouse Reservation became part of the Tybee National Wildlife Refuge when it was transferred from the U.S. Coast Guard to the U.S. Fish and Wildlife Service.[5]

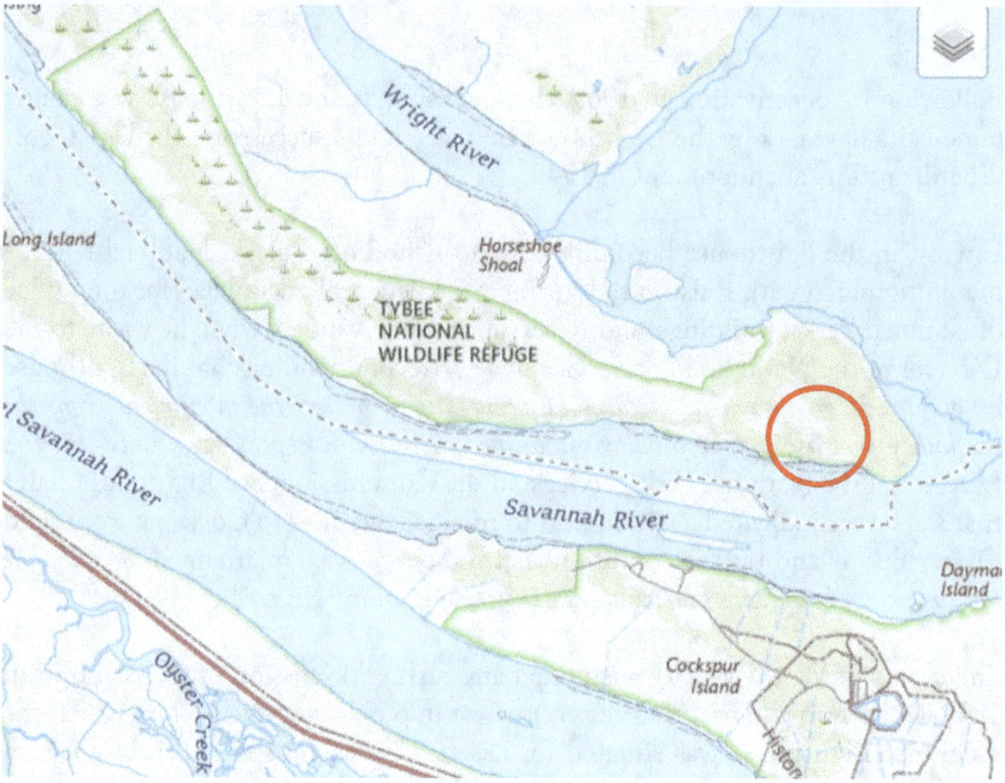

Tybee National Wildlife Refuge
This 100-acre migratory bird refuge began as a one-acre oyster shoal called Oyster Bed Island (the eastern end of the refuge). The U.S. Army Corp. of Engineers has used the shoal as a dredge spoil site since the mid-1800s. Over the decades, the accumulated spoil eventually joined Oyster Bed Island and Jones Island to form the north bank of the Savannah River. The refuge was established in 1938 with the U.S. Coast Guard (USCG) retaining control of the one-acre Oyster Bed Lighthouse Reservation. The USCG transferred the "Day Beacon Tower" and site to the U.S. Fish and Wildlife Service in 1960.[6] *Image courtesy of the USGS.*

In 1960 the National Park Service began the first of several restorations of the Cockspur Island Lighthouse. For decades the little lighthouse was a popular destination for day-trippers who crossed over to the islet by boat to climb the stairs and enjoy the view. Over the years wear and tear from day-trippers, vandals, and nature began to take its toll on the beacon, which bears the brunt of approaching tropical storms and constantly rising sea levels as a result of its location at the mouth of the Savannah River. The destructive effects of rising sea levels and tides have been exacerbated over the decades by the regular dredging of the Savannah River. In addition, ill-conceived repairs made during the mid-20th century also contributed to the deterioration of the masonry structure.[7] By the early 1990s, the Cockspur Lighthouse was in need of a major restoration.

In 1995 plans were made for an extensive restoration of the lighthouse, beginning with the original cast-iron lantern. The lantern was removed in 1997 to begin electrolysis repair – a process that would take several years. During this time the masonry interior of the lighthouse was exposed and open to the elements. While the lantern was being restored, several storms damaged the masonry exterior and interior of the lighthouse. In 1998, large waves from Tropical Storm Earl buffeted the seaward side of the beacon, damaging a 10-foot section of the "keel" while the exposed masonry in the lantern room suffered extensive damage resulting in the partial collapse of the brick parapet that supports the cast iron lantern room. In 1999, unusually high tides associated with another storm washed away the exterior stairs. During the Winter of 1999, a team of masons from the Historic Preservation Training Center (HPTC) – working with Fort Pulaski staff, reconstructed the damaged section of the keel, rebuilt the exterior stairs, repaired the brick parapet in the lantern room, and repaired cracks within the interior of the tower. While this work was being conducted, it was determined that the deterioration of the original cast iron lantern was too severe to be properly restored. As a result, a replica of the original lantern was commissioned and installed in May of 2000.[8]

The completion of the restoration campaign was celebrated with a re-lighting ceremony in 2007. Working in conjunction with the Coast Guard and the newly formed "Friends of the Cockspur Island Lighthouse" (FOCIL), National Monument staff installed a solar powered lantern in the lighthouse, which was relit in a formal ceremony on March 18th, 2007.[9]

In 2008, the Georgia Trust for Preservation – Georgia's only state-wide historic preservation organization, placed the Cockspur Island Lighthouse on its annual "Places in Peril" list, despite its recent restoration. The justification for including the lighthouse on the list was based on the accelerated erosion of the islet in which its sited – due to the ongoing dredging of the Savannah River, and the threat to the beacon from natural and man-made forces associated with increased traffic. Later that same year, the beacon's timber "grillage" foundation was treated for an infestation of shipworms that was discovered by members of the Southeast Archeological Center.[10]

Increased awareness of the ongoing conservation issues facing the stewards of the Cockspur Island Lighthouse resulted in the appropriation of $1.5 million through the office of U.S. Congressman Jack Kingston to fund the construction of a granite revetment around the lighthouse to combat further erosion of the island and to protect the lighthouse itself. Working with Park Service staff, the U.S. Corp of Engineers began the revetment project in November of 2012.[11] It was completed in late January of 2013.

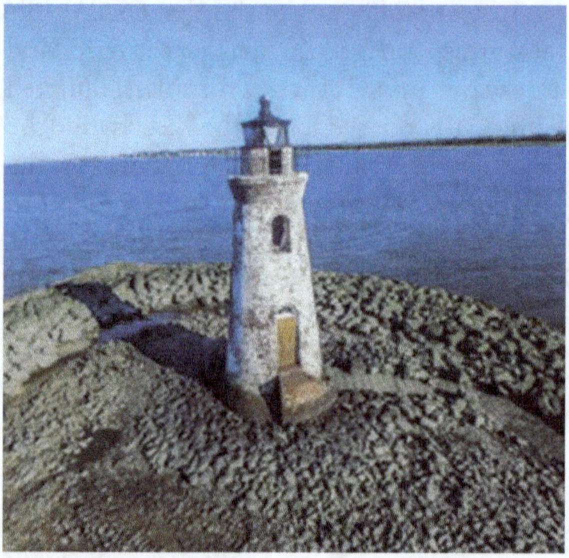

Cockspur Island Lighthouse c2020
Photograph courtesy of Savannah Port Journal

During the revetment project large granite stones were placed in a semi-circular ring around the lighthouse, beginning at the northwest corner and extending eastward to the southeast corner of the island, leaving the western portion open. The project was designed to protect the lighthouse from direct impact from wave action as well as decrease the effects of erosion on the surrounding islet. The revetment also provided the additional benefit of eliminating accessibility to the islet by larger boats, limiting visitor traffic as a whole.[12]

Cockspur Point Revetment Project c2012 – *Photograph courtesy of Allen Lewis.*

Taken from the lighthouse, this photo provides a view southwest of crews building the concrete block walkway and stone revetment along the South Channel side of the islet. The revetment forms a "breakwater" protecting the islet and lighthouse from the powerful wake of the cargo ships passing daily up the Savannah River. The west end of the islet remains open providing limited access by small boat. Due to ongoing preservation efforts, the lighthouse and islet are currently closed to the public. However, visitors can get a closer look at the lighthouse from the Lighthouse Overlook Trail.

Cockspur Point c2021 – *Photograph courtesy Frank Logue*

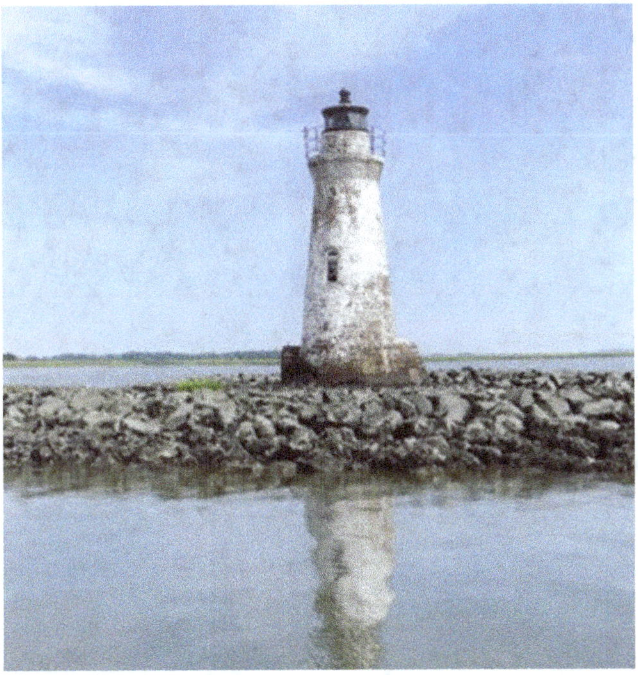

Cockspur Island Lighthouse c2021
View northeast, taken before the masonry repair project. *Photograph courtesy FOCIL*

In 2021 the reopening of the Lighthouse Overlook Trail coincided with the beginning of a new $150,000 restoration project to address deferred work on the masonry exterior and interior of the lighthouse. A recently completed observation deck at the end of the trail allowed visitors to observe the work being conducted.

During the project, the masonry tower, stairs, keel, window and door openings, and interior of the lighthouse were cleaned, chiseled, and re-pointed. Other work included replacing the deteriorated windows and door to match the materials and configuration of what was installed originally with the exception of the fanlights above the doors and windows – louvered transoms were installed to allow for passive ventilation through the structure. Funding for the fabrication of the door and windows was provided by a grant given to the Friends of the Cockspur Lighthouse (FOCIL) by the Tybee Island Historical Society, which was matched by NPS Centennial Challenge Funding.

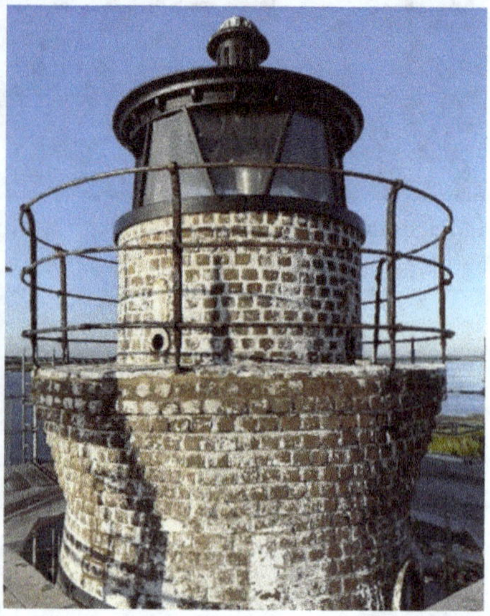

Cockspur Island Lighthouse c2021
View north of scaffolding around the lighthouse during the brick re-pointing project. Detail view of lantern room and gallery. *Photos courtesy of the National Park Service*

Cockspur Island Lighthouse c2021
Taken from the observation deck at the end of the Lighthouse Overlook Trail, this photo provides a view east of the scaffolding installed around the lighthouse during the 5-month long masonry repointing project. *Photograph courtesy of the National Park Service*

Interior Stairs - Cockspur Island Lighthouse
View of the interior brick stairs that lead to the wood frame floor of the second level of the lighthouse.
Photograph courtesy of FOCIL

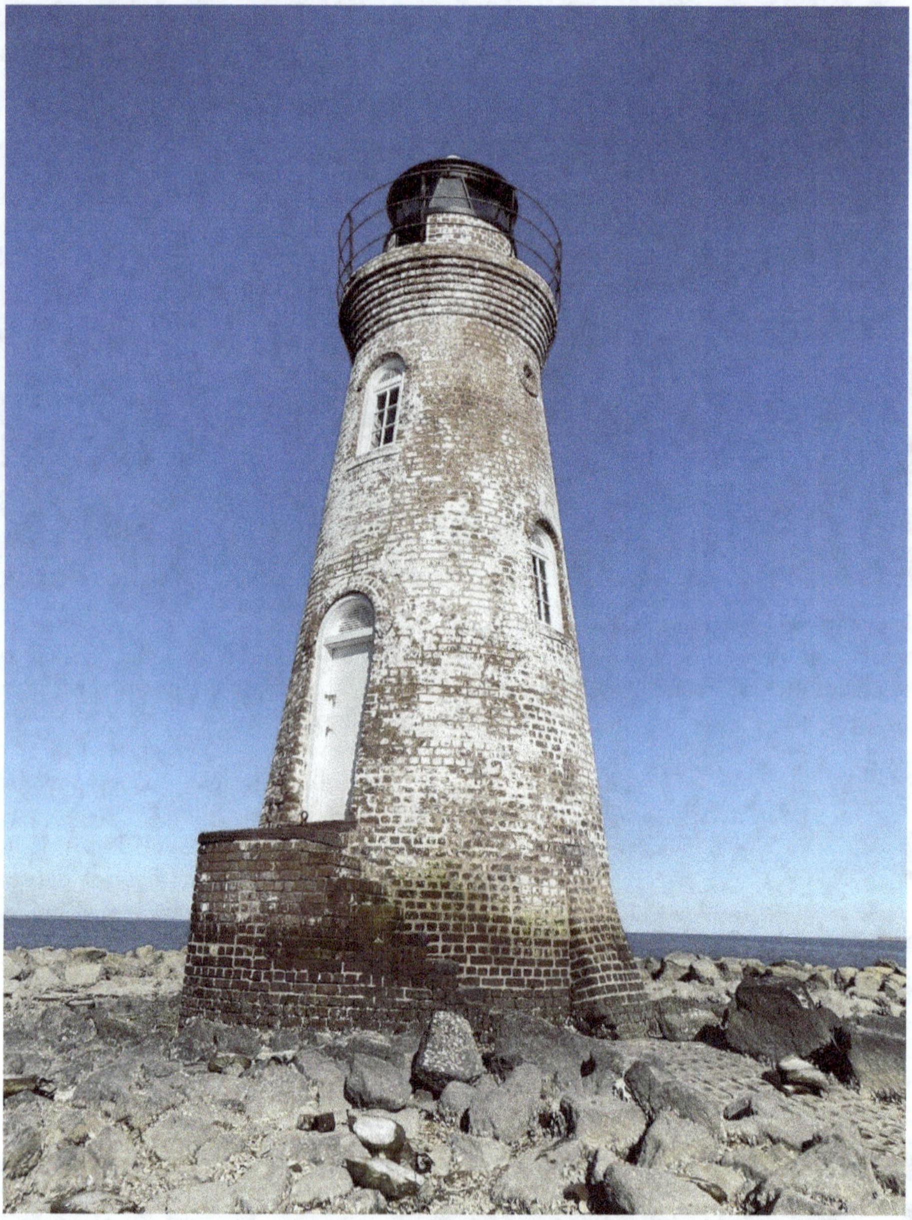

Cockspur Island Lighthouse "Day Mark"
In order to make lighthouses recognizable to mariners during the day, the towers were given a distinctive paint scheme, or "day mark." The day mark of the Cockspur Island Lighthouse is white, which was assigned to the beacon in 1866. Currently, an improperly applied coat of latex paint from an earlier repair project prevents the repainting of the lighthouse to its historically-accurate hue. Painting over the latex would suffocate and damage the masonry even more than various methods of physical or chemical removal – park staff has determined that the best and safest way to remove the coating is to let it wear away naturally.[13] *Photograph courtesy of Fort Pulaski Monument*

Chapter One - The Island

1. Lou Grohl, "Cultural Overview: Fort Pulaski National Monument." National Park Service. Last modified February 12, 2000, https://www.nps.gov/orgs/1539/the-southeast-chronicles-fort-pulaski-national-monument.htm
2. J. Faith Meador, "Fort Pulaski National Monument Administration History" (Atlanta, GA, National Park Service, 2003), p. 3.
3. Robert A. Ciucevich, Tybee Island: The Long Branch of the South. (Charleston: Arcadia Publishing, 2005), p. 14
4. Grohl, "Cultural Overview: Fort Pulaski National Monument."
5. Patti Babin, Peter Russell, and Megan Zida, "Fort Pulaski North Pier," HALS No. GA-9, Historic American Landscape Survey (HALS"), National Park Service, U.S. Department of the Interior, 2022, p. 6.
6. Grohl, "Cultural Overview: Fort Pulaski National Monument."
7. Ibid.
8. Ciucevich, Tybee Island: The Long Branch of the South, p.15-16.
9. Babin, "Fort Pulaski North Pier," p 7.
10. Grohl, "Cultural Overview: Fort Pulaski National Monument."
11. Babin, "Fort Pulaski North Pier," p 7.
12. "The Second System of Seacoast Fortifications," National Park Service, April 14, 2015. https://www.nps.gov/fosu/learn/historyculture/second-system-forts.htm
13. Babin, "Fort Pulaski North Pier," p 7.
14. Grohl, "Cultural Overview: Fort Pulaski National Monument."
15. Babin, "Fort Pulaski North Pier," p 7 & 8.
16. Grohl, "Cultural Overview: Fort Pulaski National Monument."
17. Ciucevich, Tybee Island: The Long Branch of the South, p. 23.
18. Ibid, p 23 – 32.
19. Ibid, p.23 – 32.
20. Ibid, p. 27.
21. "Enslaved to Soldier on the Georgia Coast." National Park Service, December 2, 2024. https://www.nps.gov/articles/000/enslaved-to-soldier-on-the-georgia-coast.htm
22. Julie de Chantal, Heidi Moye, Anastatia Sims, "African Americans at Fort Pulaski, 1733 – 1900: A Special History Study," National Park Service, U.S. Department of Interior, 2022, p 67-84.
23. "Enslaved to Soldier on the Georgia Coast."

24. "History of the Fort Pulaski Workers Village," National Park Service, February 12, 2024. https://www.nps.gov/fopu/learn/historyculture/workersvillage.htm)
25. Ibid.
26. Ralston B. Lattimore, Fort Pulaski National Monument, Georgia, Handbook Series No. 18 (Washington, D.C., National Park Service, 1954, Reprint 1961), p. 42.
27. Tommy H. Jones, Fort Pulaski National Monument Quarantine Attendants Quarters Historic Structures Report, (Atlanta, GA: National Park Service, 2004), p. 11 – 31.
28. Grohl, "Cultural Overview: Fort Pulaski National Monument."
29. "Quarantine Station – Fort Pulaski National Monument," National Park Service, December 29, 2024. https://www.nps.gov/articles/000/quarantine-station.htm
30. Ciucevich, Tybee Island: The Long Branch of the South, p 33.
31. Ibid, p 34.
32. Ibid, p 34 - 35.
33. Ibid, p 35.
34. Lattimore, Fort Pulaski National Monument, Georgia, p 43.
35. Jones, Fort Pulaski National Monument Quarantine Attendants Quarters Historic Structures Report, p 11 – 31.
36. Ibid, p 14.
37. Ibid, p 16 – 17.
38. Ibid, p 38.
39. Ibid, 17- 18.

Chapter Two - The Lighthouse

1. Lou Grohl, "Cultural Overview: Fort Pulaski National Monument." National Park Service. Last modified February 12, 2000, https://www.nps.gov/orgs/1539/the-southeast-chronicles-fort-pulaski-national-monument.htm
2. Maria Vincent, "Cockspur Island Lighthouse," United States Coast Guard, July 23, 2019. https://www.history.uscg.mil/Browse-by-Topic/Assets/Land/All/Article/1912752/cockspur-island-lighthouse/
3. Historic American Buildings Survey (HABS), Cockspur Island Lighthouse, HABS No. GA-2265, Washington, D.C.: Department of the Interior, 1980, p. 2.
4. Grohl, "Cultural Overview: Fort Pulaski National Monument."
5. HABS, Cockspur Island Lighthouse, p 2.
6. Ibid, p. 3
7. Kraig Anderson, "Cockspur Island Lighthouse," Lighthouse Friends, 2025, https://www.lighthousefriends.com/light.asp?ID=324
8. HABS, Cockspur Island Lighthouse, p 4.
9. Ibid, p 4.
10. Edward L. Trout, "Fort Pulaski National Monument," National Register of Historic Places Nomination Form (Washington, D.C.: U.S. Department of the Interior, National Park Service, 1974).
11. HABS, Cockspur Island Lighthouse p 8 -11.
12. Ibid, p 8.
13. "The United States Lighthouse Board of 1852," Fenwick Island Lighthouse, 2008, https://fenwickislandlighthouse.org/united-states-lighthouse-board/
14. Josh Liller, "Bright Ideas #5: Daniel Woodbury and Standard Lighthouse Design, United States Lighthouse Society, September 5, 2020, https://news.uslhs.org/2020/09/03/bright-ideas-5-daniel-woodbury-and-standard-lighthouse-design/
15. George W. Cullum, Biographical Register of the Officers and Graduates of the United States Military Academy at West Point, New York since 1802," Vol. I, p 740. Updated December 5, 2013. https://penelope.uchicago.edu/Thayer/E/Gazetteer/Places/America/United_States/Army/USMA/Cullums_Register/989*.html
16. Julie de Chantal, Heidi Moye, and Anastatia Sims, "African Americans at Fort Pulaski, 1733 – 1900: a Special History Study," National Park Service, U.S. Department of Interior, 2022, p 75.

CHAPTER THREE - GEORGIA'S LIGHTHOUSES

1. Unites States Light-house Board, Annual Report of the Light-House Board of the United States to the Secretary of the Treasury for the Fiscal Year Ended .... United States: U.S. Government Printing Office, 1855.
2. Russ Rowlett, "The Oldest U.S. Towers, 1764 – 1791," The Lighthouse Directory, September 21, 2018, https://www.ibiblio.org/lighthouse/types/oldest.html
3. Ibid.
4. Russ Rowlett, "Early Federal Octagonals, 1792 – 1817," The Lighthouse Directory, September 22, 2018, https://www.ibiblio.org/lighthouse/types/octagonals.html
5. Cullen Chambers, A Brief History of the Tybee Island Light Station: 1732 - 1999, (Tybee Island: Tybee Island Historical Society, 1999), p 10 -11.
6. Rowlett, "Early Federal Octagonals."
7. Ibid. / Kraig Anderson, "Georgia Lighthouses," Lighthouse Friends, 2001-2025. https://www.lighthousefriends.com/pull-state.asp?state=GA&Submit=Go
8. Russ Rowlett, "Old Style Brick Lighthouses, 1820 – 1849," The Lighthouse Directory, September 23, 2018, https://www.ibiblio.org/lighthouse/types/oldstylebrick.html
9. Ibid.
10. Buddy Sullivan, "The Lighthouses of Georgia," The Keeper's Log, U.S. Lighthouse Society, Spring 1988, p 6., chrome-extension://efaidnbmnnnibpcajpcglclefindmkaj/https://uslhs.org/sites/default/files/articles_pdf/Lighthouses%20of%20Georgia.pdf
11. Russ Rowlett, "Early Classic Brick Towers," The Lighthouse Directory, October 3, 2018, https://www.ibiblio.org/lighthouse/types/earlymodernbrick.html
12. Josh Liller, "Bright Ideas #5: Daniel Woodbury and Standard Lighthouse Design," United States Lighthouse Society, September 5, 2020, https://news.uslhs.org/2020/09/03/bright-ideas-5-daniel-woodbury-and-standard-lighthouse-design/
13. Sullivan, "The Lighthouses of Georgia," p 10. Kraig Anderson, "Little Cumberland Island, Lighthouse, GA," Lighthouse Friends, 2001-2025, https://www.lighthousefriends.com/light.asp?ID=329
14. Sullivan, "The Lighthouses of Georgia," pp. 2 – 11. Anderson, "Georgia Lighthouses."
15. Rowlett, "Old Style Brick Lighthouses."
16. Lillet, "Bright Ideas #5."
17. Rowlett, "Old Style Brick Lighthouses."
18. Kraig Anderson, "Sapelo Island Lighthouse," Lighthouse Friends, 2001-2015, https://www.lighthousefriends.com/light.asp?ID=326

19. Rowlett, "Early Classic Brick Towers."
20. Ibid.
21. Lillet, "Bright Ideas #5."
22. Rowlett, "Old Style Brick Lighthouses."
23. Sullivan, "The Lighthouses of Georgia," pp. 2 – 11. Anderson, "Georgia Lighthouses."
24. Chambers, A Brief History of the Tybee Island Light Station," pp. 1 – 11.
25. Sullivan, "The Lighthouses of Georgia," pp. 7 – 10.
26. Wayne Wheeler, "Little Known Lighthouses: The Portland Breakwater Light Station," The Keepers Log, U.S. Lighthouse Society, Spring 2004, chrome-extension://efaidnbmnnnibpcajpcglclefindmkaj/https://uslhs.org/sites/default/files/articles_pdf/portland_breakwater.pdf

CHAPTER FOUR - THE LIGHT STATION

1. Kraig Anderson, "Cockspur Island Lighthouse," Lighthouse Friends, 2001-2015 https://www.lighthousefriends.com/light.asp?ID=324
2. Rita DeLorme, "Light Keepers Log: Early Keepers of the Cockspur Light," The Southern Cross, September 28, 2007, p 3.
3. Historic American Buildings Survey (HABS), Cockspur Island Lighthouse, HABS No. GA-2265, Washington, D.C.: Department of the Interior, 1980, p. 4.
4. DeLorme, "Light Keepers Log: Early Keepers of the Cockspur Light." "History of the Cockspur Island Lighthouse," Friends of the Cockspur Island Lighthouse (FOCIL), 2015, https://cockspurislandlighthouse.com/
5. George W. Cullum, Biographical Register of the Officers and Graduates of the United States Military Academy at West Point, New York since 1802," Vol. I, p 740. Updated December 5, 2013. https://penelope.uchicago.edu/Thayer/E/Gazetteer/Places/America/United_States/Army/USMA/Cullums_Register/989*.html
6. Unites States Light-house Board, Annual Report of the Light-House Board of the United States to the Secretary of the Treasury for the Fiscal Year Ended .... United States: U.S. Government Printing Office, 1855.
7. Kraig Anderson, "Fig Island Range Lighthouse," Lighthouse Friends, 2001-2015 https://www.lighthousefriends.com/light.asp?ID=1854
8. Annual Report of the Light-house Board, 1855.
9. Anderson, "Cockspur Island Lighthouse."
10. "Cockspur Island Lighthouse," National Park Service, June 4, 2016, https://www.nps.gov/fopu/learn/historyculture/cockspur-light.htm
11. Lou Grohl, "Cultural Overview: Fort Pulaski National Monument," National Park Service. Last modified February 12, 2000, https://www.nps.gov/orgs/1539/the-southeast-chronicles-fort-pulaski-national-monument.htm
12. HABS, Cockspur Island Lighthouse, pp 4 – 5.
13. Anderson, "Cockspur Island Lighthouse."
14. Ibid.
15. DeLorme, "Light Keepers Log: Early Keepers of the Cockspur Light," p 3.
16. Unites States Light-house Board, Annual Report of the Light-House Board of the United States to the Secretary of the Treasury for the Fiscal Year Ended .... United States: U.S. Government Printing Office, 1875 - 1909.
17. Anderson, "Cockspur Island Lighthouse."

18. Annual Report of the Light-House Board, 1875.
19. Annual Report of the Light-House Board, 1879.
20. Annual Report of the Light-House Board, 1886.
21. Annual Report of the Light-house Board, 1874.
22. Annual Report of the Light-house Board, 1876.
23. Annual Report of the Light-house Board, 1878.
24. Kraig Anderson, "Tybee Island Lighthouse," Lighthouse Friends, 2001-2015 https://www.lighthousefriends.com/light.asp?ID=322
25. Annual Report of the Light-house Board, 1877 – 1879.
26. Anderson, "Cockspur Island Lighthouse."
27. HABS, Cockspur Island Lighthouse, p 5./ DeLorme, "Light Keepers Log: Early Keepers of the Cockspur Light," p 3.
28. Annual Report of the Light-house Board, 1882.
29. Ibid.
30. Anderson, "Cockspur Island Lighthouse."
31. Annual Report of the Light-house Board, 1884.
32. Kraig Anderson, "Parris Island Lighthouse," Lighthouse Friends, 2001-2015 https://www.lighthousefriends.com/light.asp?ID=868
33. Kraig Anderson, "Venus Point Lighthouse," Lighthouse Friends, 2001-2015 https://www.lighthousefriends.com/light.asp?ID=1862
34. Anderson, "Cockspur Island Lighthouse."
35. Annual Report of the Light-house Board, 1886.
36. Annual Report of the Light-house Board, 1887.
37. Kraig Anderson, "Elba Island Range Lighthouse," Lighthouse Friends, 2001-2015 https://www.lighthousefriends.com/light.asp?ID=1853
38. Annual Report of the Light-house Board, 1893, 1896, 1898.
39. Annual Report of the Light-house Board, 1890.
40. Eric S. Blake, Christopher W. Landsea, Ethan J. Gibney, "The Deadliest, Costliest and Most Intense Unites States Tropical Cyclones from 1851 to 2010," National Hurricane Center, National Oceanic and Atmospheric Administration (NOAA), August 10, 2011, Preface, chrome-extension://efaidnbmnnnibpcajpcglclefindmkaj/https://www.nhc.noaa.gov/pdf/nws-nhc-6.pdf
41. DeLorme, "Light Keepers Log: Early Keepers of the Cockspur Light," p 3.
42. Annual Report of the Light-house Board, 1893.
43. "USLHT Pharos," NavSource Online: Lighthouse Tender Photo Archives, 1996 – 2025, https://www.navsource.org/archives/12/179744.htm
44. Douglas Peterson, United States Lighthouse Service Tenders: 1840 – 1939, Annapolis: Eastwind Publishing, 2000.
45. Anderson, "Cockspur Island Lighthouse."

46. Annual Reports of the Light-house Board, 1905 – 1909.
47. Buddy Sullivan, "The Lighthouses of Georgia," The Keeper's Log, U.S. Lighthouse Society, Spring 1988, p 5., chrome-extension://efaidnbmnnnibpcajpcglclefindmkaj/https://uslhs.org/sites/default/files/articles_pdf/Lighthouses%20of%20Georgia.pdf
48. HABS, Cockspur Island Lighthouse, p 5.
49. Ibid, p 5.
50. Kraig Anderson, "Kraig Anderson Inventory of Lighthouse Personnel," United States Lighthouse Society, October 30, 2018, https://archives.uslhs.org/people/gustaf-ohman

Chapter Five - The Keepers

1. Unites States Light-House Board, Annual Report of the Light-House Board of the United States to the Secretary of the Treasury for the Fiscal Year Ended .... United States: U.S. Government Printing Office, 1881 – 1884.
2. Kraig Anderson, "Kraig Anderson Inventory of Lighthouse Personnel," United States Lighthouse Society, October 30, 2018, https://archives.uslhs.org/people
3. Candace Clifford, "Researching Lighthouse Keepers," Lighthouse History, March 2015, https://lighthousehistory.wordpress.com/2015/03/26/researching-light-house-keepers/
4. Candace Clifford, "Keeper Job Descriptions," Lighthouse History, November 4, 2013, https://lighthousehistory.wordpress.com/2013/11/04/keeper-job-descriptions/
5. Dennis L. Noble, Lighthouses and Keepers: The U.S. Lighthouse Service and its Legacy, (Annapolis: Naval Institute Press, 1997), pp 87-88.
6. Annual Report of the Light-house Board, 1852.
7. "United States Lighthouse Board of 1852," Fenwick Island Lighthouse, https://fenwickislandlighthouse.org/united-states-lighthouse-board/
8. Noble, Lighthouses and Keepers, pp. 88.
9. Office of the Light-house Board, Instructions for Lighth-Keepers of the United States, Treasury Department, Washington, D.C., 1852. Office of the Light-house Board, Instructions for Light-Keepers, Treasury Department, Washington, D.C., July 1881.
10. Noble, Lighthouses and Keepers, pp. 88.
11. Anderson, "Inventory of Lighthouse Personnel,"
12. George Worthtylake, "The Keeper's New Clothes," The Keeper's Log, U.S. Lighthouse Society, Fall 2001, chrome-extension://efaidnbmnnnibpcajpcglclefindmkaj/https://uslhs.org/sites/default/files/articles_pdf/keepers_new_clothes.pdf
13. J. Candace Clifford, Cullen Chambers, and Robert A. Ciucevich, "Tybee Island Light Station," National Register of Historic Places Nomination Form (Washington, D.C.: U.S. Department of Interior, National Park Service, 2018), pp 6 – 10.
14. "Paul J. Pelz," Wikipedia, February 26, 2025, https://en.wikipedia.org/wiki/Paul_J._Pelz#References
15. Kraig Anderson, "Cape Fear Lighthouse," Lighthouse Friends, 2001-2025 https://www.lighthousefriends.com/light.asp?ID=350
16. Noble, Lighthouses and Keepers, p. 90.
17. "The Lightkeepers," Cape Hatteras National Seashore, National Park Service, October

29, 2017, https://www.nps.gov/caha/learn/historyculture/lightkeepers.htm

18. "Explore the Ponce Inlet Light Station," Ponce de Leon Inlet Lighthouse and Museum, 2024, https://www.ponceinlet.org/tour-explore/explore-the-museum/explore-the-ponce-inlet-light-station/
19. Richard Cloues, "Fort Screven Historic District," National Register of Historic Places Nomination Form (Washington, D.C.: U.S. Department of Interior, National Park Service, 1982).
20. Office of the Light-house Board, Instructions and Directions for Light Keepers, Government Printing Office, Washington, D.C., September 1871.
21. Ibid, p. 17.
22. Ibid,
23. "Fresnel Lens Orders, Sizes, Weights, . . ." U.S. Lighthouse Society, 2023, https://uslhs.org/node/1427
24. "Life in a Lighthouse," Clarke Historical Library, Central Michigan University, undated, https://www.cmich.edu/research/clarke-historical-library/explore-collection/explore-online/michigan-material/lighthouses/life-in-a-lighthouse
25. 1850 U.S. Federal Census, District 13, Chatham County, Georgia.
26. 1890 and 1900 U.S. Federal Census, District 13, Chatham County, Georgia.
27. Kraig Anderson, "Kraig Anderson Inventory of Lighthouse Personnel," United States Lighthouse Society, October 30, 2018, https://archives.uslhs.org/people/1920 U.S. Federal Census, District 13, Chatham County, Georgia.
28. "United States Lighthouse Board of 1852."
29. 1850 U.S. Federal Census/Anderson, "Cockspur Island Lighthouse"
30. Noble, Lighthouses and Keepers, pp. 98 – 101.
31. Ibid, p 98.
32. "United States Lighthouse Board of 1852,"
33. Kraig Anderson, "Kraig Anderson Inventory of Lighthouse Personnel," United States Lighthouse Society, October 30, 2018, https://archives.uslhs.org/people/1850, 1860, & 1870 U.S. Federal Census, District 13, Chatham County, Georgia.
34. 1850 U.S. Federal Census
35. Ralston B. Lattimore, Fort Pulaski National Monument, Georgia, Handbook Series No. 18 (Washington, D.C., National Park Service, 1954, Reprint 1961), pp 54 – 55./ 1870 U.S. Federal Census
36. J. Faith Meador, "Fort Pulaski National Monument Administration History" (Atlanta, GA, National Park Service, 2003), p. 13.
37. Anderson, "Cockspur Island Lighthouse"
38. "U.S., Returns from Military Posts, 1806 – 1916", National Archives and Records Administration, April 1879. / Meador, "Fort Pulaski National Monument Administration History," p 13.

39. Anderson, "Cockspur Island Lighthouse"
40. Ibid/Sholes, A.E.. "Volume VIII, Sholes' Directory of the City of Savannah, 1886."
41. "Miss Florence Martus, Famed as 'Waving Girl,' Dies in Savannah," The Bulletin (Augusta, Ga.), February 27, 1943, p. 8.
42. "The Lone Light House Girl: Story of Miss Martus and Her Life on Elba Island," Savannah Morning News, January 31, 1904, p 10.
43. Ibid, p 10.
44. "Always Remember the River Queen as You Sail By," The Baltimore Sun, November 12, 1911, Part 4, p 8. / "Savannah Girl In Part of Heroine," The Augusta Herald (Augusta, Ga.), October 26, 1911, p. 14.
45. "Celebration: Florence Martus," National Park Service, undated, https://www.nps.gov/media/photo/view.htm?id=66E9C1DD-32A9-4D94-A991-836A63645C05
46. Noble, Lighthouses and Keepers, pp. 103 – 109.
47. Mary Louise Clifford and J. Candace Clifford, Women Who Kept the Lights, (Cypress Communications; 2nd edition, January 1, 2001).
48. Noble, Lighthouses and Keepers, p 109.
49. Kelsey Chander, "Women Who Kept the Lights," Interpretive Marker, Tybee Island Historical Society, 2025.
50. "History of the Fort Pulaski Workers Village," National Park Service, February 12, 2024. https://www.nps.gov/fopu/learn/historyculture/workersvillage.htm
51. Chandler, "Women Who Kept the Lights."
52. Ibid / Anderson, "Anderson Inventory of Lighthouse Personnel"

Chapter Six - The Daymark

1. Lou Grohl, "Cultural Overview: Fort Pulaski National Monument." National Park Service. Last modified February 12, 2000, https://www.nps.gov/orgs/1539/the-south-east-chronicles-fort-pulaski-national-monument.htm
2. Historic American Buildings Survey (HABS), Cockspur Island Lighthouse, HABS No. GA-2265, Washington, D.C.: Department of the Interior, 1980, p. 5-6.
3. Ibid, pp 7-8.
4. Grohl, "Cultural Overview: Fort Pulaski National Monument."
5. "Tybee National Wildlife Refuge," State of Georgia Parks, 2025, https://stateparks.com/tybee_national_wildlife_refuge_in_georgia.html
6. Ibid
7. Stephen E. Hartley and Paul Hardin Kapp, " Moisture Analysis and P, reservation Practice at Cockspur Island Lighthouse in Georgia," APT Bulletin: The Journal of Preservation Technology 51, NO. 2/3 (2020): p. 66.
8. Stephen E. Hartley and Paul Hardin Kapp, Cockspur Island Lighthouse Historic Structures Report, (Atlanta, GA: National Park Service, 2016), pp. 3-4
9. "About the Friends of the Cockspur Island Lighthouse," Friends of the Cockspur Island Lighthouse (FOCIL), 2015, https://cockspurislandlighthouse.com/
10. Hartley, Cockspur Island Lighthouse Historic Structures Report, pp. 5-6.
11. Ben Goggins, "Cockspur Lighthouse Counting on Friends," Savannah Morning News, April 23, 2019, p. B6
12. Hartley, Cockspur Island Lighthouse Historic Structures Report, pp. 7-8.
13. Phil Gast, "Cockspur Lighthouse Emerges From Scaffolding after Months of Preservation Work," The Civil War Picket, November 17, 2012. https://civil-war-picket.blogspot.com/2021/11/cockspur-lighthouse-at-fort-pulaski.html

INDEX

Photograph courtesy of the Friends of Cockspur Island Lighthouse

About the Friends of Cockspur Island Lighthouse

The Friends of Cockspur Island Lighthouse (FOCIL) was established in 2007 to act in unison with the National Park Service (NPS) in its efforts to preserve this important coastal landmark. The group has fostered a strong bond with NPS staff at Fort Pulaski National Monument in its efforts to raise awareness of the conservation challenges facing this significant beacon and to assist in its preservation. FOCIL's role as a vocal public advocate for the conservation of the Cockspur Lighthouse has facilitated the assistance of Congressional leaders and other stakeholders in its role as a conduit for receiving and directing private funds and grants to directly benefit NPS efforts to preserve the lighthouse for future generations.

FOCIL began in 2004 with a conversation between two friends – C. Harvey Ferrelle III and John C. Wylly, Jr. Both men realized that the Cockspur Island Lighthouse was in a need of advocacy if it was to persevere. Enlisting the help of Charlie Fenwick, Superintendent of the Fort Pulaski National Monument, and noted lighthouse preservationist Cullen Chambers, Executive Director of the Tybee Island Historical Society, the seeds of FOCIL were sown. Other significant early contributors include Mike and Norma McKinley. Mike – a retired judge, did much of the legal paperwork to establish FOCIL and – along with Norma, made up the backbone of the organization's early efforts. The McKinleys provided much needed financial support through the McKinley Preservation Fund, which they established

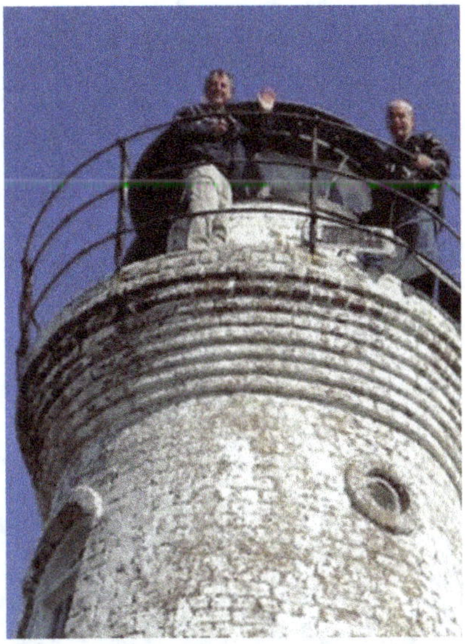

Early FOCIL board member **Cullen Chambers** (waving) atop the Cockspur Island Lighthouse.

to assist in the preservation of the Cockspur Island Lighthouse. Allied with the McKinleys in those earlier days was Howard J. Morrison, Jr. Howard brought his passion for Savannah history and his experience serving on many educational and charitable boards to FOCIL and became a driving force in helping craft a vision for moving forward. Another key contributor was Keith Noerenberg. As president of the "North Georgia Beacon Brigade" – a group that raised money for lighthouse preservation, Keith and several fellow members made significant early financial contributions to help fund various FOCIL projects. These are just a few of the numerous board members and volunteers who have dedicated hundreds of hours helping FOCIL in its efforts over the years.

The Friends of the Cockspur Island Lighthouse is a Not For Profit 501 3(c) entity. This book represents the latest efforts by FOCIL to raise awareness of the significance of the lighthouse and its vital role in Savannah's maritime history. All proceeds from the sale of this book will benefit future efforts of the Friends of the Cockspur Island Lighthouse.

If you would like to become a member of FOCIL, please visit:

www.CockspurIslandLighthouse.com.

Photograph courtesy of Sharon Lindsay

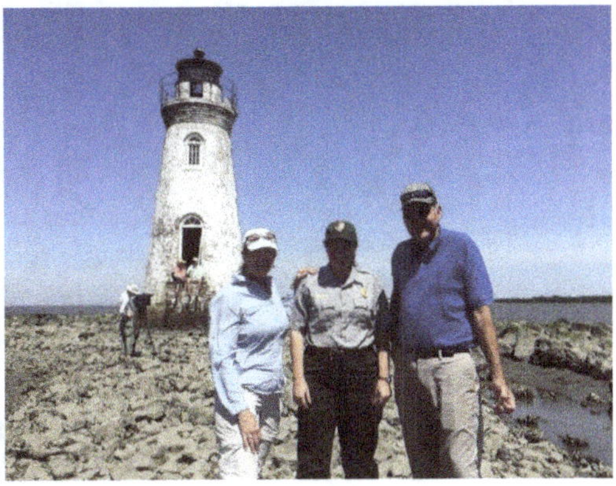

Clockwise from bottom:
Poster for FOCIL's annual jamboree; Fort Pulaski staff and FOCIL members discuss conservation efforts onsite at the Cockspur Lighthouse; Fort Pulaski staff repairing the masonry steps of the lighthouse; Board members Cathy Sakas and John Wylly, Jr. pose with Melissa Memory, Superintendent of Fort Pulaski National Monument – Harvey Ferrelle III and Sharon Collins in the background being interviewed by Georgia Public Broadcasting (GPB); Allen Lewis giving a tour (below).

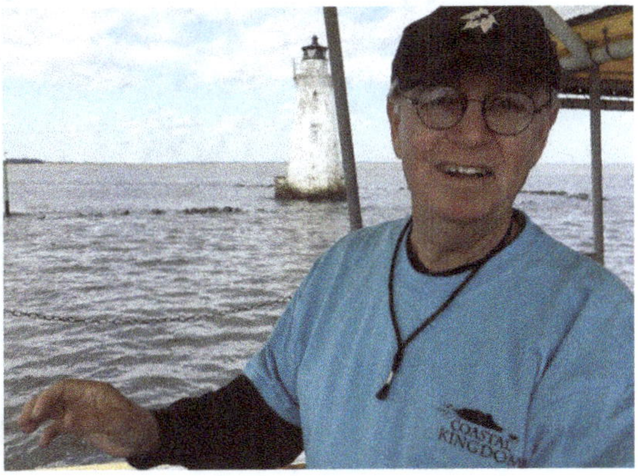

Friends of the Cockspur Island Lighthouse Board Members

Officers

C. Harvey Ferrelle III – President
Cathy J. Sakas – Vice President
William (Bill) Cliett, Jr. – Treasurer
Liz Hood – Secretary

At Large Members

Kate Burns
Allen Lewis
Ralph Maggioni
Debbie Meeks
Mark Padgett
Chuck Powell
Karen Robertson
Nick Sears
Sam Shay
Trey Thompson III
John C. Wylly, Jr.
Joe Brennan *(In Memoriam)*
Jane Bridges *(In Memoriam)*

Honorary Board Members

Captain Gary "Gator" Hill
Derek Brown, Derek's Dolphin Tours

Sweet Lowland

It's not one of my blind creations - I've been there it feels like heaven
She walks among SUN SEA and SAND.

Chorus:
So turn on the light at Cockspur Island
Lead me through Lazaretto
I want to go home Sweet Lowland.

I'd spend my life counting the raindrops on her face and when the rain stops
We'll walk among SUN SEA and SAND

So turn on the light at Cockspur Island
Lead me through Lazaretto - I want to go home
Sweet Lowland

Next time you sleep
You might dream her - then you'll see why I need her
And you'll walk among SUN SEA and SAND

Chorus:
So turn on your light at Cockspur Island
Lead me through Lazaretto
I want to go home Sweet Lowland.

Words and Music: Dodd Inglesby Ferrelle
Copyright Lighthouse Music 2002

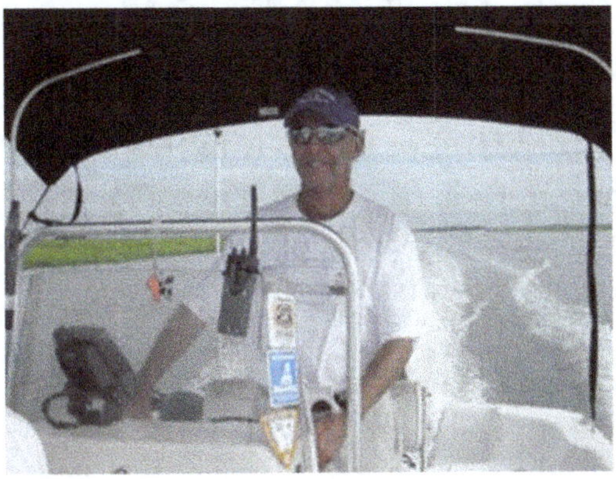

Captain C. Harvey Ferrelle III (at left) of Sweet Lowland Tybee Tours. Harvey's son Dodd penned the song "Sweet Lowland," which he performed during the 2007 relighting ceremony, the historical marker unveiling, and at other FOCIL events. The proceeds from the sale of Dodd's CD raised over $3,000 earmarked for FOCIL projects.

The Friends of the Cockspur Island Lighthouse Board wish to thank the City of Tybee, its council members, and mayor for funding the research, writing and production of *The Cockspur Island Lighthouse: A Witness to History.*

The Honorable Brian West, Mayor of the City of Tybee Island

Tybee Island City Council

Kathryn Williams

Nick Sears

Michael "Spec" Hosti

Monty Parks

Bill Garbett

Tony Ploughe

The Friends of the Cockspur Island Lighthouse would like to thank our Congressional delegation for its support and assistance, especially former U.S. Congressman Jack Kingston – who was instrumental in securing a $1.5 million dollar allocation to fund the stone revetment that protects the lighthouse and Cockspur Point, and to U.S. Congressman Buddy Carter – who has actively supported FOCIL's efforts by facilitating and advising on available grants and advocating for projects conducted by the Corps of Engineers that benefit the preservation of the Cockspur Lighthouse. The office of Senator Raphael Warnock, State Representatives Jesse Petrea and Ben Watson, and Chatham County Commissioner Pat Farrell have all offered their assistance and support – FOCIL thanks you.

The Friends of the Cockspur Island Lighthouse would also like to thank Sarah Jones – Executive Director of the Tybee Island Historical Society (TIHS), for all her assistance over the years – especially her efforts in facilitating a major grant for the production and installation of windows and a door for the lighthouse as well as allowing the sale of FOCIL items in the TIHS giftshop.

FOCIL is fortunate to have the assistance of so many talented collaborators, for which they offer a grateful thank you: Sharon Collins of Georgia Public Broadcasting for raising awareness of the Cockspur Lighthouse in the documentary *The Lighthouse*; film maker Michael Jordan for his early assistance in creating FOCIL documentaries; author and photographer David Zapatka for including outstanding photos of the Cockspur Lighthouse in his book "Stars and Lights: Darkest of Dark Nights;" Professors Steven H. Hartley and Paul H. Kapp for their outstanding work in preparing the *Cockspur Island Lighthouse Historic Structures Report*, which provided the blueprint for past and future preservation work; and "honorary board members" Captain Gary "Gator" Hill and Derek Brown of Derek's Dolphin Tours. Captain Hill has made the Cockspur Lighthouse a centerpiece of their tours - raising donations for and awareness of the lighthouse and of FOCIL's efforts, while Derek is an annual sponsor of the FOCIL Jamboree, which is held at Derek's wharf at Lazaretto Creek.

Captain Gary "Gator" Hill

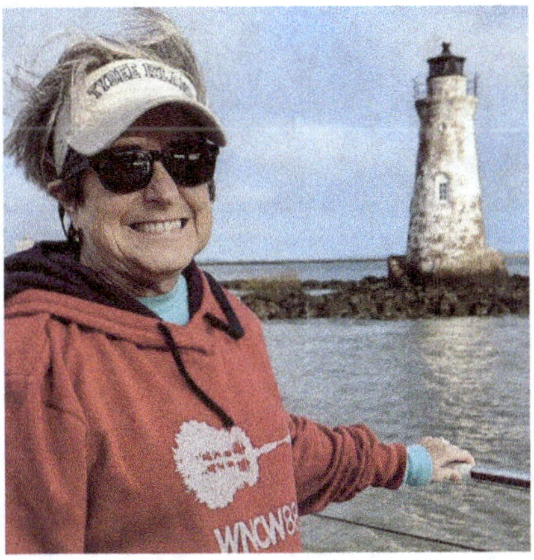

Jane Bridges

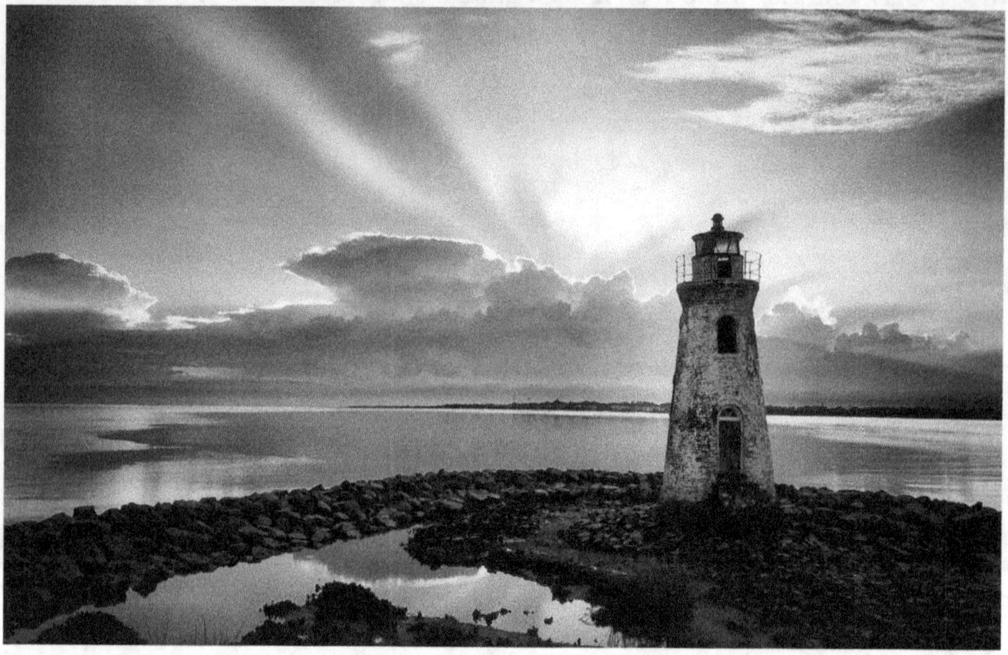

Photograph courtesy of Frank Logue

On behalf of The Friends, a personal ***THANK YOU*** to all those supporters from Tybee, Savannah and beyond that have remained loyal and faithful to our efforts.

Both with financial contributions, buying memberships and moral support throughout the last 20 years. Some of you are recognized with a placard on a plaque in the Ft. Pulaski visitors center.

BTW the journey has only just begun so please continue to remember us and our preservation efforts that you are so much a part of.

Thank you,

C. Harvey Ferrelle III

Founding Director and President
The Friends of Cockspur Island Lighthouse

John C. Wylly Jr.

Founding Director
The Friends of Cockspur Island Lighthouse

Photograph courtesy of Frank Logue

FRIENDS OF COCKSPUR ISLAND LIGHTHOUSE, GEORGIA

www.ingramcontent.com/pod-product-compliance
Lightning Source LLC
Chambersburg PA
CBHW081536120626
46550CB00009B/2751
9781959563419